AF594555

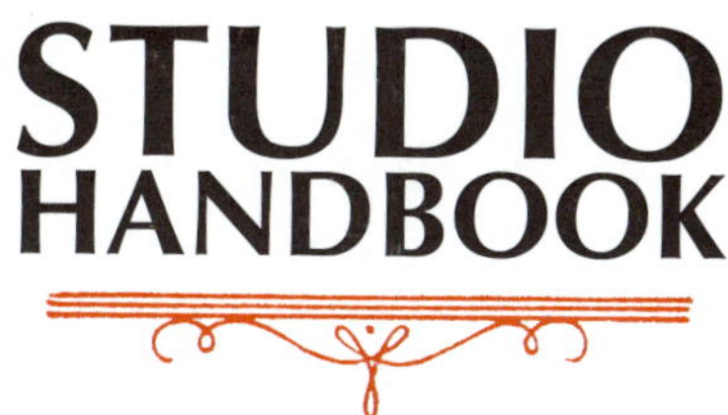

LETTERING & DESIGN
NEW ENLARGED EDITION

SAMUEL WELO

DOVER PUBLICATIONS, INC.
MINEOLA, NEW YORK

Bibliographical Note

This Dover edition, first published in 2017, is an unabridged republication of the work originally published in 1931 by Frederick J. Drake & Co., Chicago, under the title *Studio Handbook: Letter & Design: New Enlarged Edition.*

Library of Congress Cataloging-in-Publication Data

Names: Welo, Samuel, author.
Title: Studio handbook : lettering & design / Samuel Welo.
Other titles: Studio handbook, letter & design
Description: New enlarged edition. | Mineola, New York : Dover Publications, 2017. | "Studio Handbook: Lettering & Design: New Enlarged Edition, first published by Dover Publications, Inc., in 2016, is an unabridged republication of Studio Handbook: Letter & Design: New Enlarged Edition, originally published by Frederick J. Drake & Co., Chicago."
Identifiers: LCCN 2016039637| ISBN 9780486811307 (hardback) | ISBN 0486811301
Subjects: LCSH: Lettering. | Alphabets. | BISAC: DESIGN / Book. | DESIGN / Graphic Arts / Advertising.
Classification: LCC NK3620 .W4 2017 | DDC 745.6/1—dc23 LC record available at https://lccn.loc.gov/2016039637

Manufactured in the United States by LSC Communications
81130101 2016
www.doverpublications.com

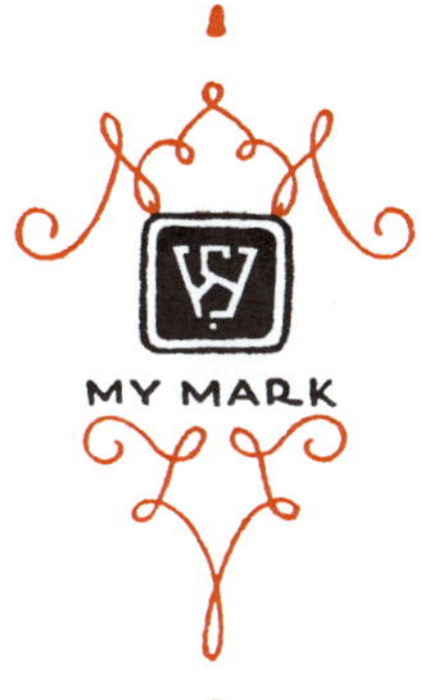
MY MARK

FOREWORD

Blessings on the heads of the Phoenecians or whoever gave us our alphabet.

Greater praise be to those who have not only made it useful but also ornamental.

Hand lettering and design will always remain an art; so this book picks up the refrain and carries it on. To professionals and amateurs, here is music for many a battle

Franklin Brucker

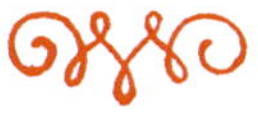

TABLE OF CONTENTS

TABLE OF CONTENTS
CONTINUED

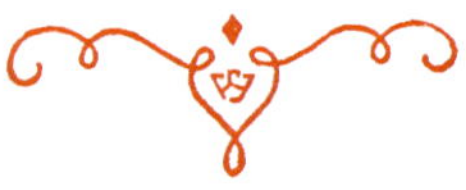

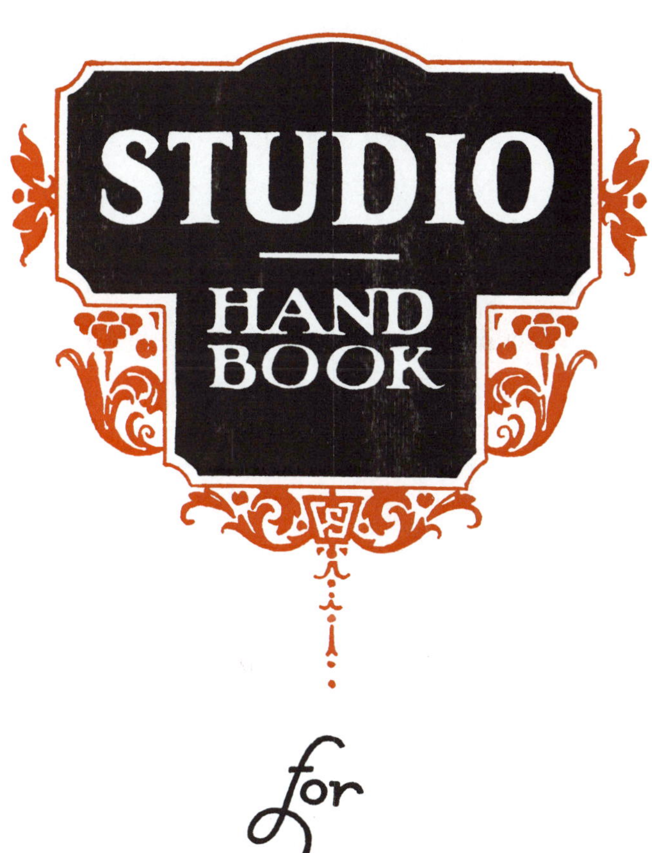

for

Artists " " "
Advertisers

Ability

The ability to draw beautifully is an accomplishment IN ITSELF

"The ability to draw plain, simple letters is an accomplishment also, But of little use without the skill to compose them effectively."

lettering

Is more than a mere side line of drawing, it is an *art* worthy of *specialization* a side line is a once in awhile but "*lettering* is now in steady -*demand*". ~~

The Massing of Letters

Improvised Letter formation for body copy paragraph or page arrangement Use full round ovals condense the vertical elements ~ ~ and a slightly broken alig~ nment adds to the unique appearance of the entire pro~ duction

Good Choice of LETTERING

To a design which requires lettering. Hand Lettering adds a grace and beauty that is as attractive as the design itself. ~ ~

Carefully ~ choose a letter to conform with the design ~ ~ ~ ~

It's the truth!

It is more difficult to design a good page of lettering than to fill the same page with a good picture

This makes the designers problem still more difficult although not hopeless

Lettering

Men that are not familiar with a certain style will not use it, hence the lack of variety

Express your thoughts and ideas in letters through wider channels and obtain variety

Every Individual

letter must have care in the making for it has as much to do with the looks of a finished word as features have to a face.

And more care should be taken in spacing of words

Hand-craft Lettering

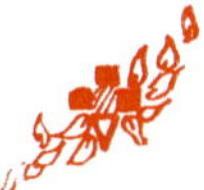

does not depend on mechanical perfection as its basic principle
Criticism consisting of individual letter analysis according to type or the standard alphabets ~ ~ would obliterate Hand Letter-craft as an applied art.
It would have no individuality and it's real value would be lost both from an artistic and commercial viewpoint ~ ~ ~ ~
However this does not mean that basic principle should be entirely sacrificed ~

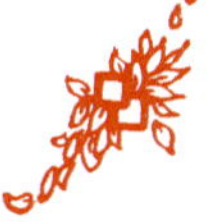

LETTERING

A Title page is an undertaking only for the most skilled
The letter should be easy to read ~
The design should have balance to please the eye ~

Modern Lettering, enlarged upon and ~ perfected through the usages of "Art" and Literature, is based on the theories of Form and Design envolved by Ancient Romans ~ in their monumental Inscriptions. yet! The Form which they attained, is unequal-ed to date ~ ~ ~ ~ ~

FSY

Be Original

Alphabets are original only so far as individual treatment and technic - alters the appearance without change of basic principle

If everything you lettered would show "individual technique", Your work would then be original and would be more in demand.

Individuality predominates

THE IMPORTANCE OF THE UNEQUAL SPACING OF CAPITALS OF IRREGULAR SHAPE IS OFTEN UNDERRATED · FAULT IS SOMETIMES FOUND WITH CAPITALS AWKWARDLY FITTED WHEN THE COMPOSITOR IS AT FAULT · · HE DOES NOT SEE THAT IT IS HIS DUTY TO RECTIFY SPACING THE GAPS PRODUCED · BY · COMBINATIONS OF · TYPE · HE DOES ALL HE CAN IN THE DESIGN AND FITTING BUT HE CANNOT MATERIALLY ALTER THE SHAPE OF AN IRREGULAR CHARACTER · · · WG

Six foremost letter Artists of today

HARVEY · H · DUNN

·D·

W. D. TEAGUE

WDT

Bertsch & Cooper

LAWRENCE L: SCHALL

-Schall-

GEO. F. TRENHOLM

GFT

GUIDO AND LAWRENCE ROSA

R+R

STUDIO Needs

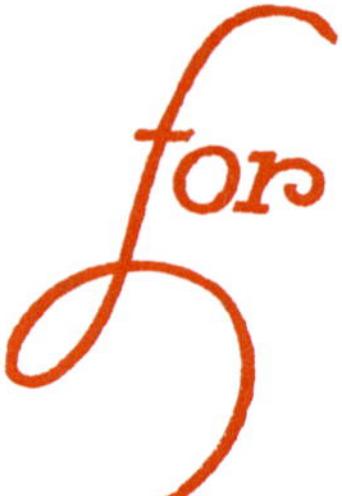

Artists and Advertisers

LETTERING

can express the following Ideas

1. Femininity
2. Antiquity
3. NOVELTY
4. Command!
5. STYLE
6. Craftsmanship
7. Conservatism
8. PERMANENCE
9. Syncopation
10. RUGGEDNESS

LETTERING
and it's meaning

OLD ROMAN

PROPRIETY

UNCIAL

SINCERITY

Gothic

DIGNITY

French Script

CAPRICE

Roman lower-case

LEGIBILITY

COMMERCIAL GOTHIC

BOLDNESS

MODERN ROMAN

MONOTONY

ART NOUVEAU

NOVELTY

WY

Lettering for Various Occasions!

The designer is often at a loss for timely lettering such as

Announcements
Greetings ~
Novelties ~
Titles ~ ~

The five pages following show fifty smart styles

WSY

Vanity Fair

Gilbert T Washburn

Wouldn't you like

For Those Who Know

Your boy needs a

Exclusive Millinery a

Eternal Freshness

Ready for Emergen

The Aluminum Six F

A Real Performer

Fifth Avenue New 6

The Watch with the

We invite mail orders and

Softest antelope leather

Costumes Tailleur

Gorham Sterling Silver

Diamond Rings 7

Great Variety

The Most Beautiful in

Three Packer Girls

WS

First Prize Panama

Good taste, guides-

Four of our buyers

Crane's Linen Lawn

Who Is Letter-Perfect In

Particularly accepta

La Femme Du Mon

Frank Waterhouser

The daintiness of a

At Thirty-Fifth Street

WV

HOLEPROOF C

Líthographs

Stephens Motor C

To your favorite Paris

Its use and enjoyments

Smart Economy

Paris Importations 15

For Everywhere

Where to Live t

We'll Rally 'Round T

WY

PIERCE-ARRO

HIGHWAY CAR

CIGARETTE SE

GRENOVILLES

WEDDING GIFTS-Illustr

ATTRACTIVE A

HAVE DECIDED VP

CRESCENT ROUTE

UNDERWOOD A

MODERN ART

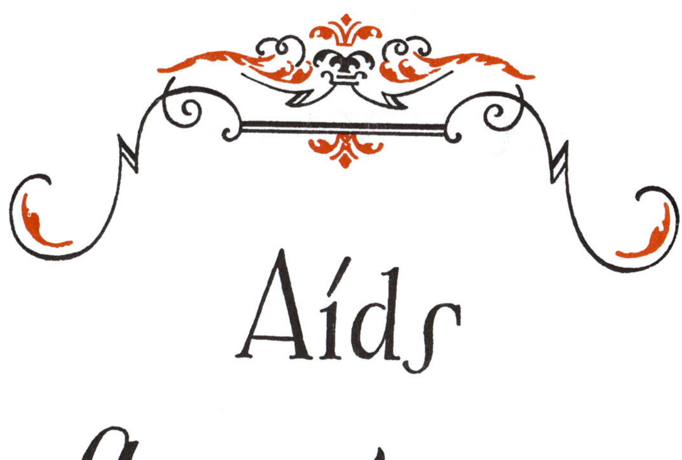

Aids *Arrangement* of LETTERING

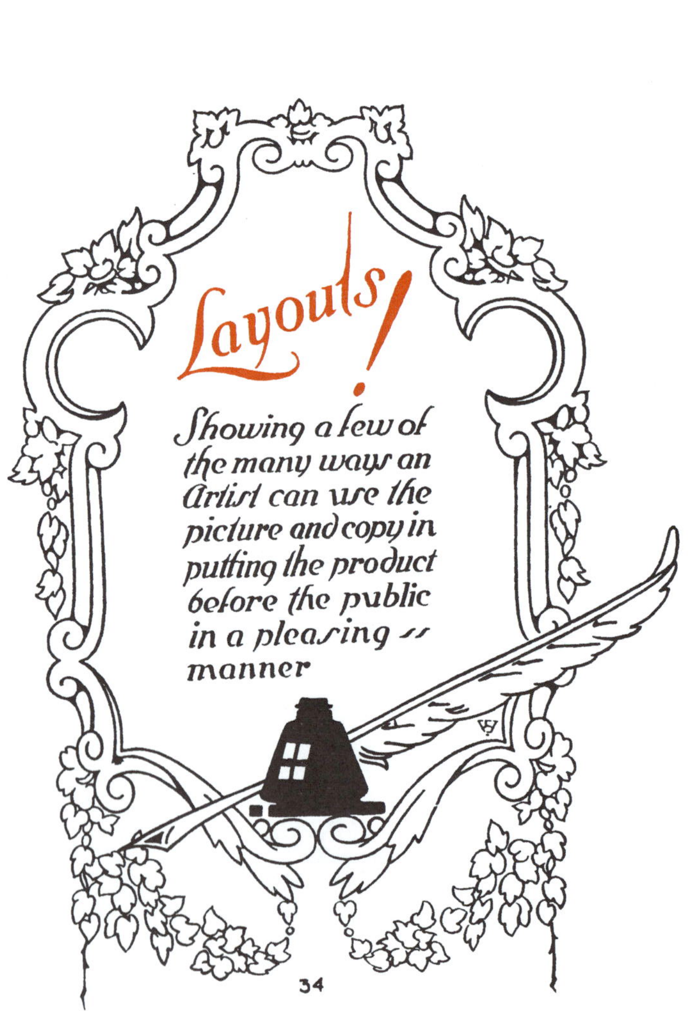
Layouts!
Showing a few of the many ways an Artist can use the picture and copy in putting the product before the public in a pleasing ,, manner

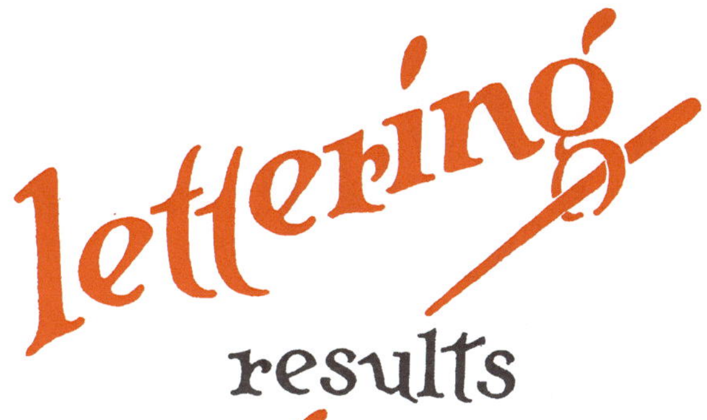

COMMANDING EFFECTS OBTAINED BY · THE · USE · OF · HAND LETTERING ADDS CHARACTER TO ANY ADVERTISING LITERATURE

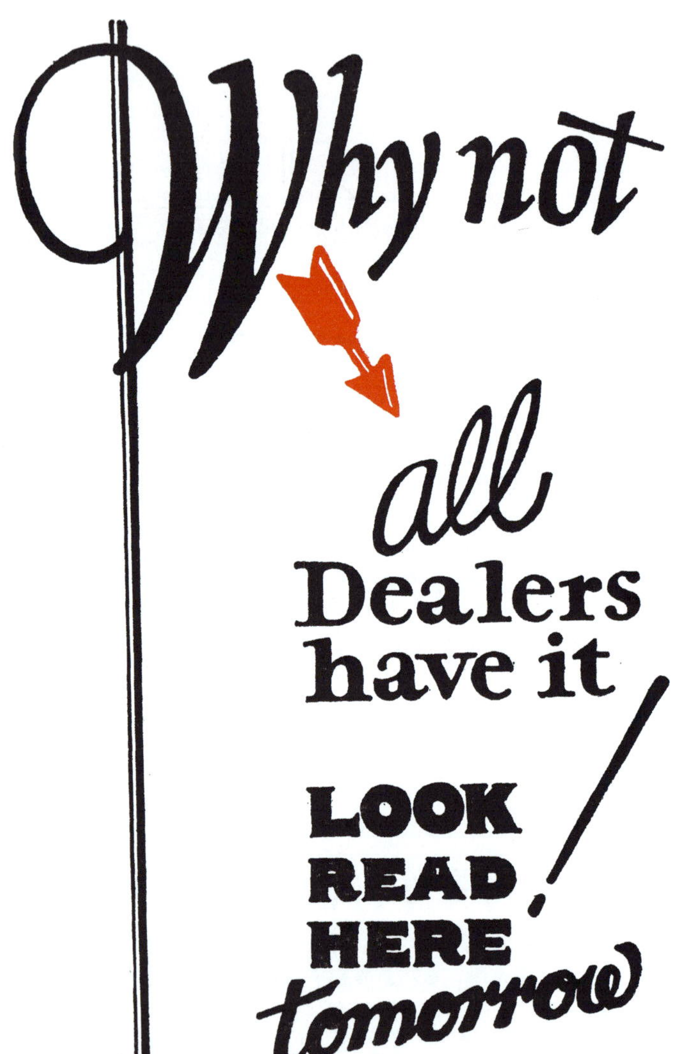
Why not
all
Dealers
have it
LOOK
READ
HERE
tomorrow

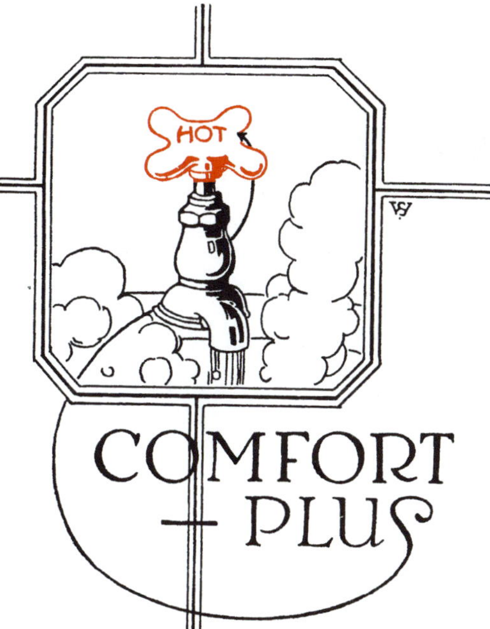

Safeguards Health and Appearance

Will you please make notation of our new address and 'phone number

ALFRED A. AUSTIN

116 WEST 32 ST ~ TELEPHONE ~
DETROIT MAIN 0505

Listening

—to the melodies of the masters

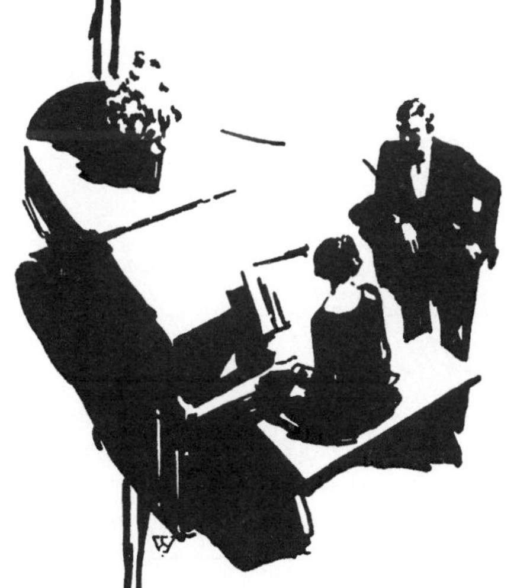

Hear it in your home

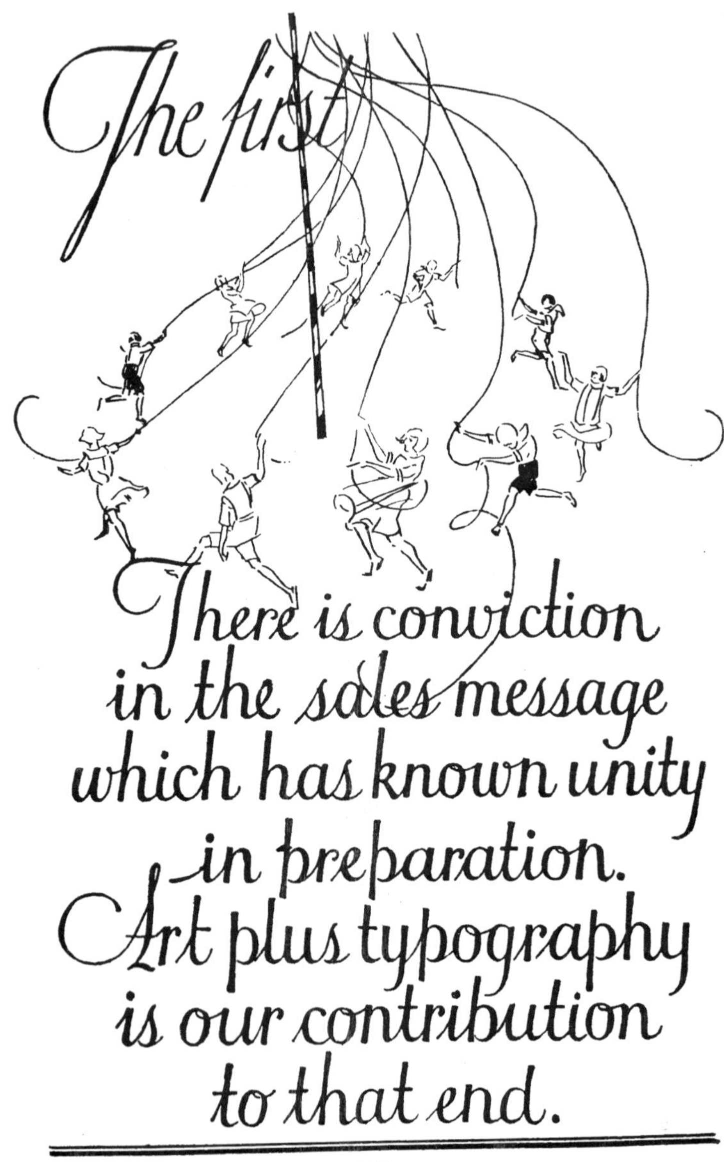
The first
There is conviction
in the sales message
which has known unity
in preparation.
Art plus typography
is our contribution
to that end.

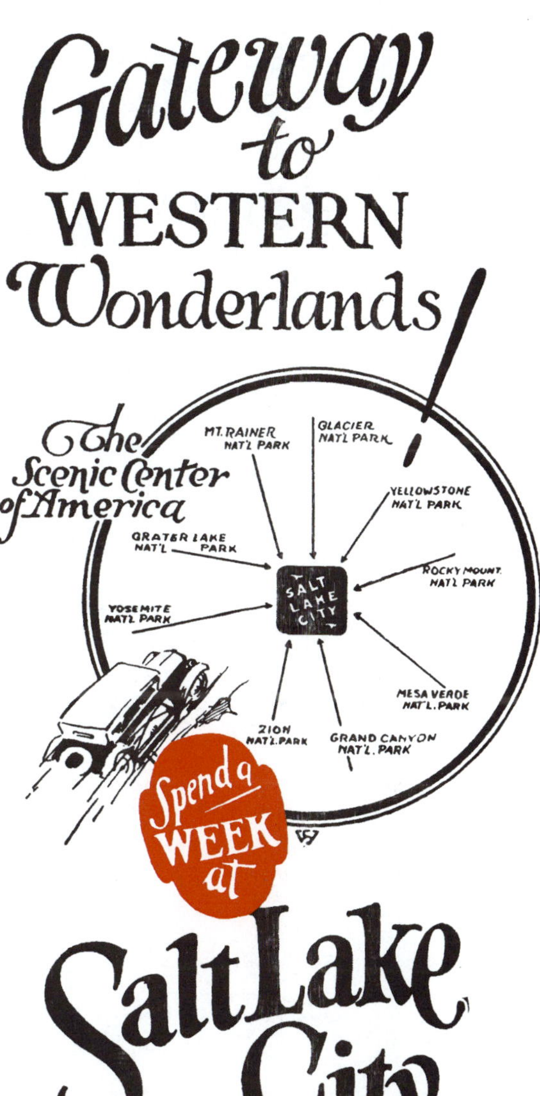
Gateway to WESTERN Wonderlands!
The Scenic Center of America
MT. RAINER NAT'L PARK
GLACIER NAT'L PARK
YELLOWSTONE NAT'L PARK
CRATER LAKE NAT'L PARK
SALT LAKE CITY
ROCKY MOUNT. NAT'L PARK
YOSEMITE NAT'L PARK
MESA VERDE NAT'L. PARK
ZION NAT'L. PARK
GRAND CANYON NAT'L. PARK
Spend a WEEK at
Salt Lake City

Composition which will carry the eye!

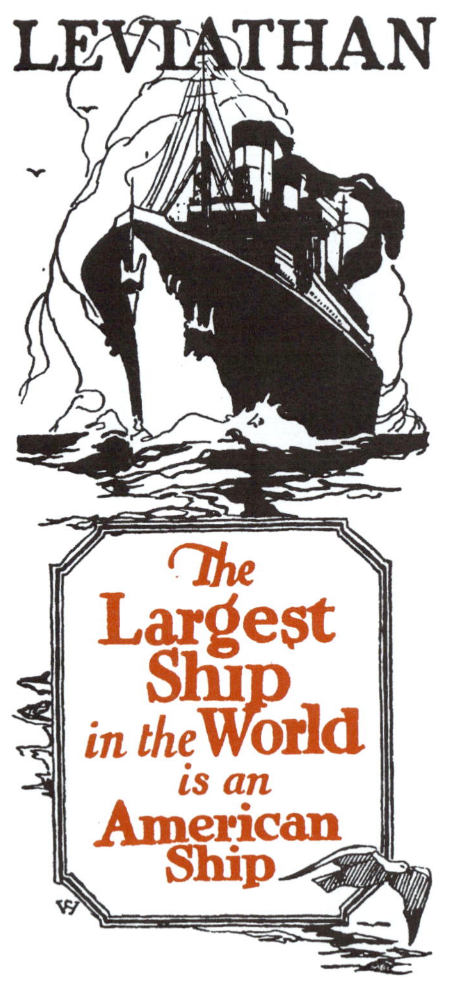

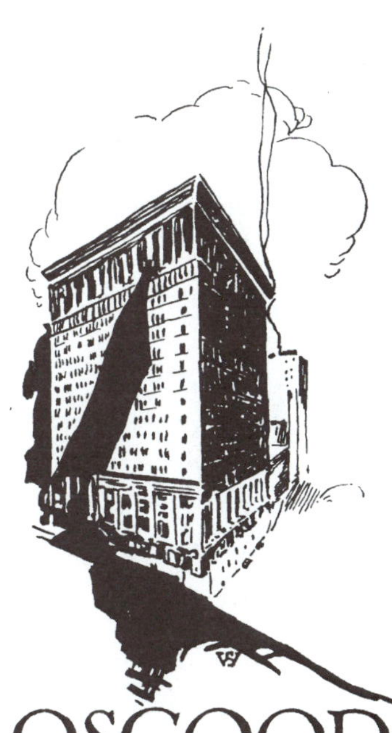

OSGOOD STUDIOS

ILLUSTRATORS *for* ADVERTISERS
COMMERCIAL PHOTOGRAPHERS
PHOTO-ENGRAVERS
COLOR PLATE MAKERS
ELECTROTYPERS-NICKELTYPERS
CATALOG-SERVICE

The Most Completely Equipped Organization of its kind in the Country

418-430 SOUTH MARKET STREET
CHICAGO

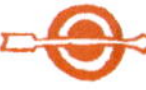
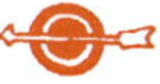

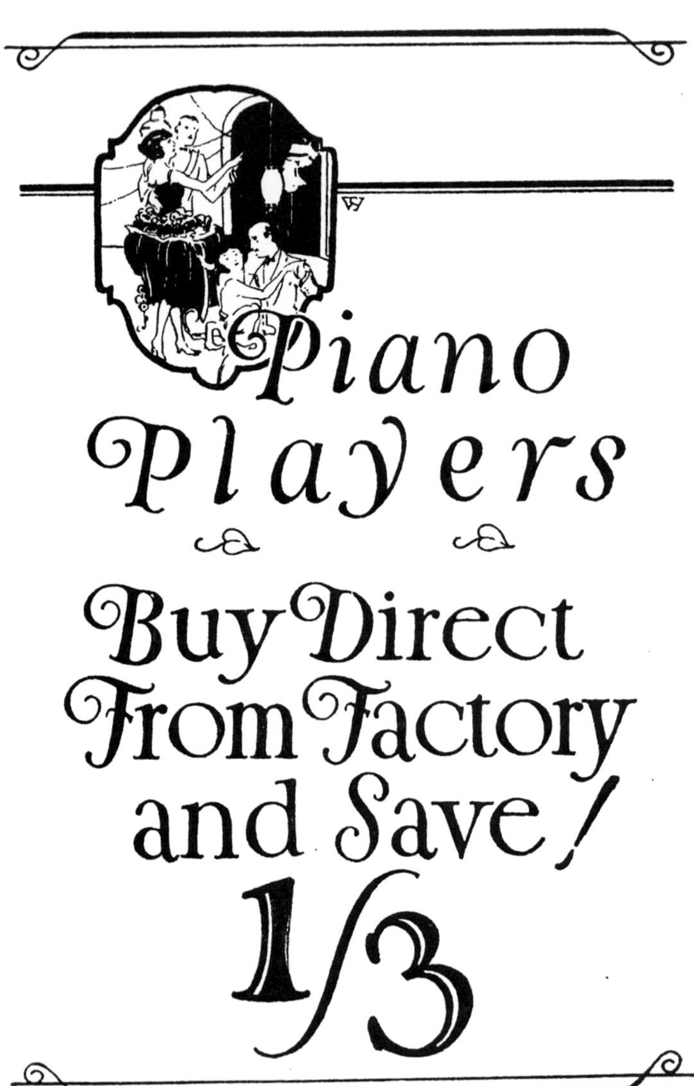
Piano
Players
Buy Direct
From Factory
and Save!
1/3

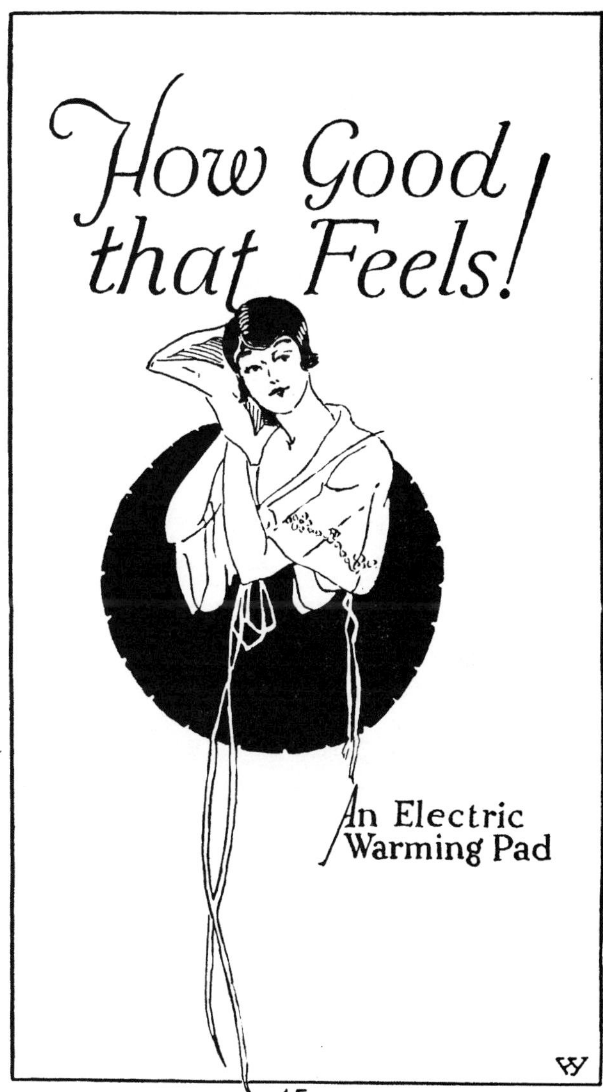
How Good that Feels!
An Electric Warming Pad
WY

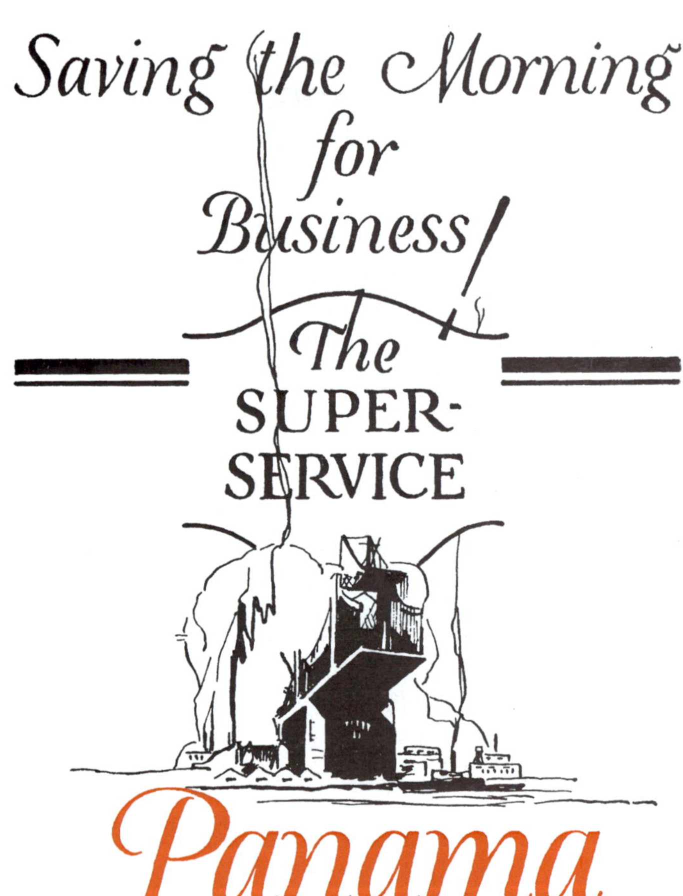
Saving the Morning
for
Business!
The
SUPER-
SERVICE
Panama

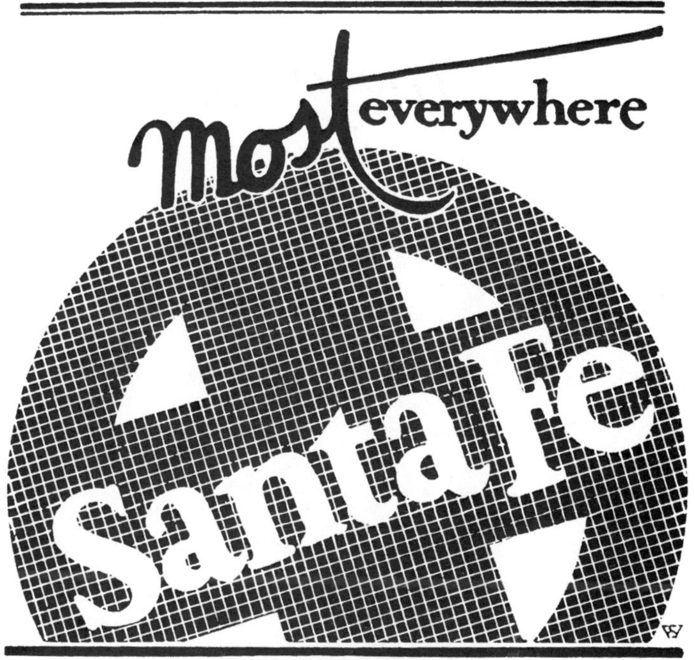

summer

Xcursions

California
Colorado
New Mexico
Arizona
and the National Parks

Fresh

CALIFORNIA

BARTLETT PEARS

NOW

for a Fresh Start

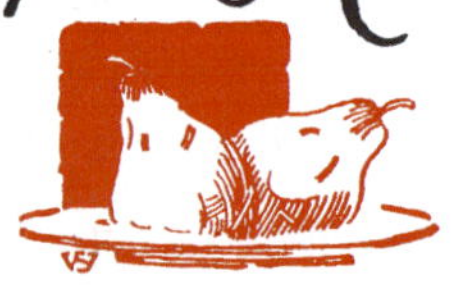

BUY THEM BEFORE THE SEASON IS GONE

buy them by the dozen

"LETTER" STRENGTH
This Shows Judgment

The first of every month will bring a check to your beneficiary as long as he or she lives —through

THE PRUDENTIAL Continuous Monthly Income Policy ~

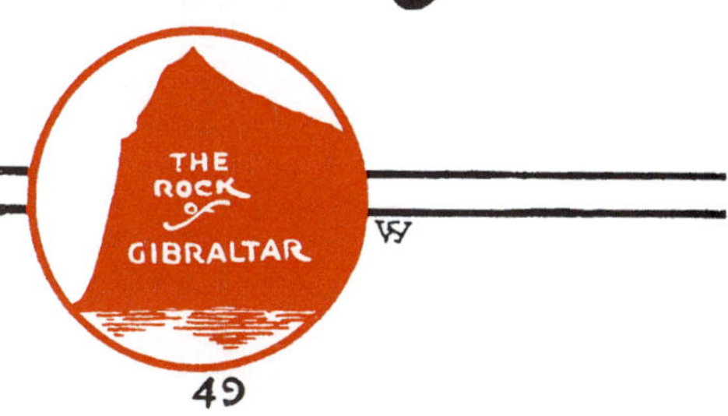

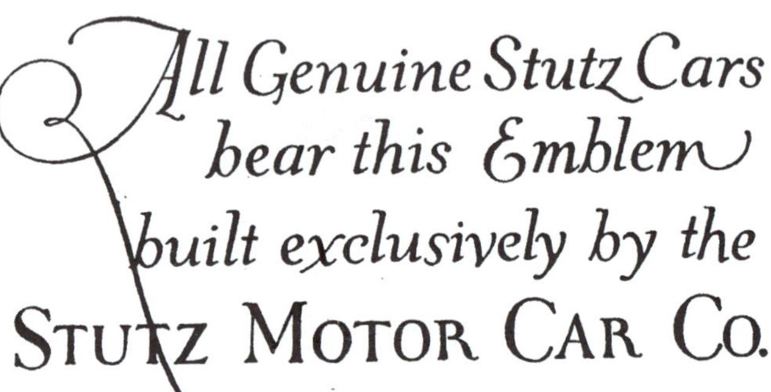

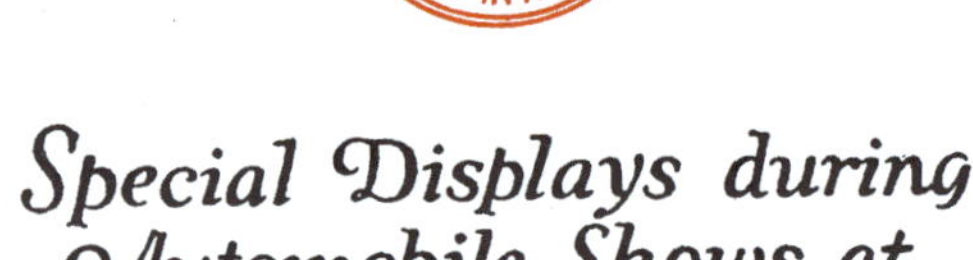

Special Displays during Automobile Shows at

Commodore Hotel. New York
New York show space B-4
Congress Hotel, Chicago
Chicago show space M-2

STUTZ MOTOR CAR CO.

Indianapolis, Indiana
U. S. A.

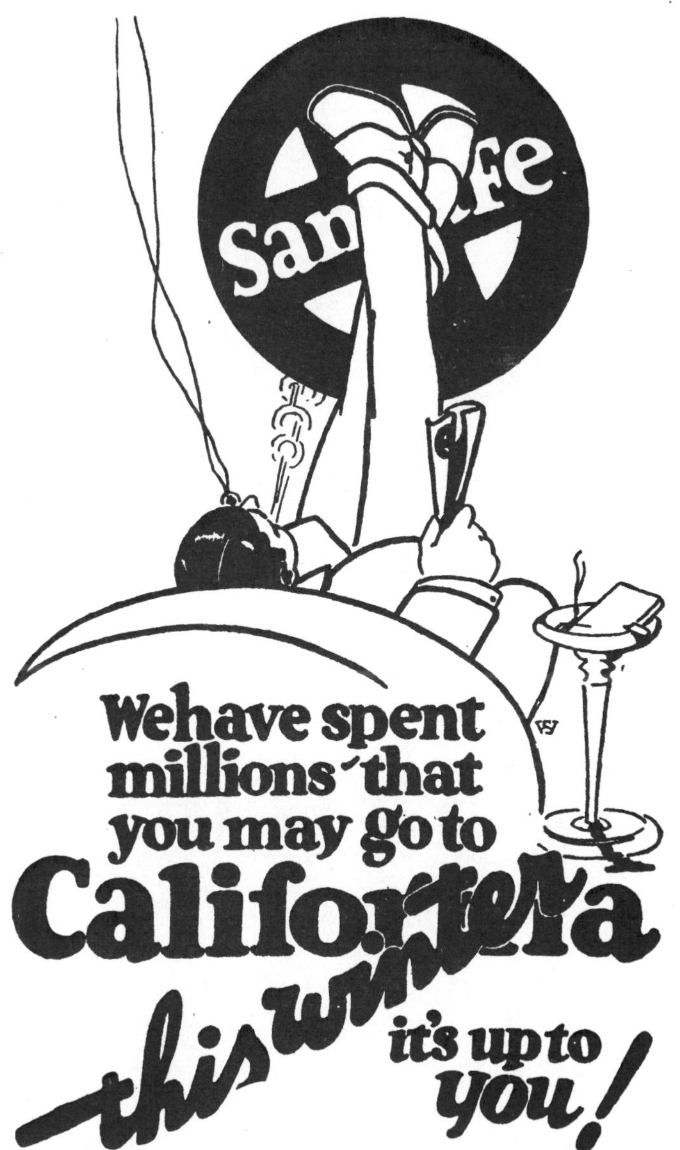
We have spent
millions that
you may go to
California
this winter
it's up to
you!

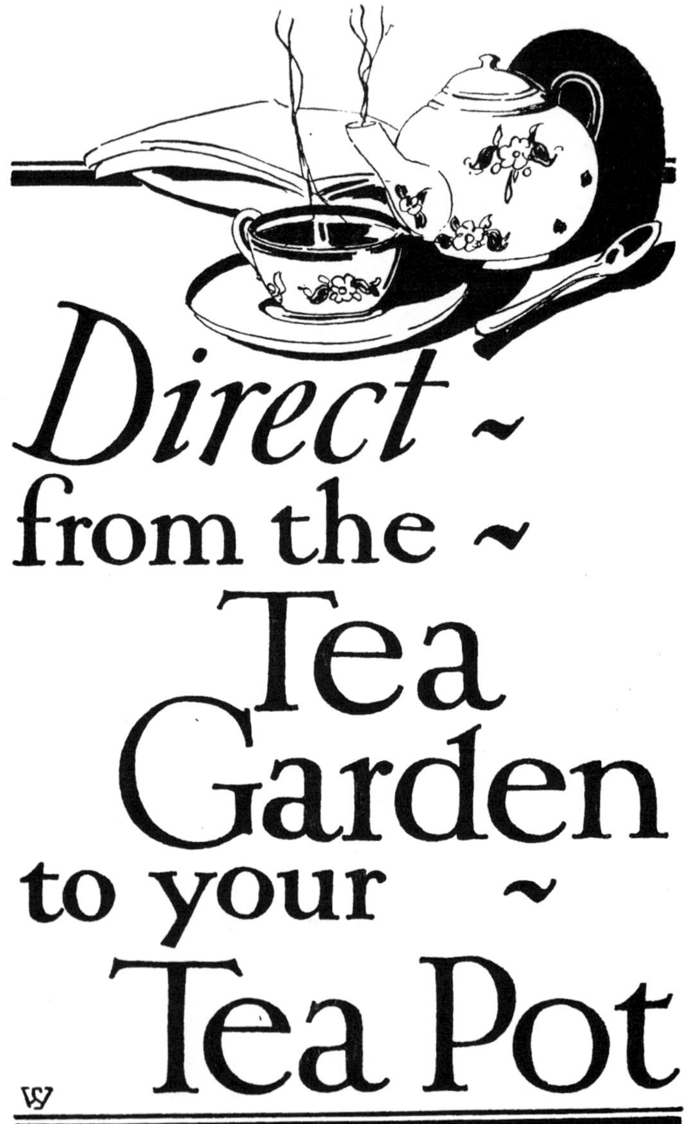
Direct ~
from the ~
Tea
Garden
to your ~
Tea Pot

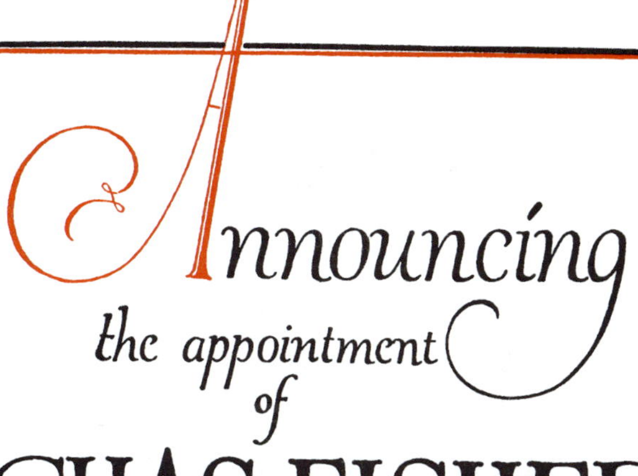

CHAS. FISHER

Advertising Manager

of

Metropolitan

Effective
September 20, 1936

A SMART
Hand-lettered Shoe Advertisment
-II-

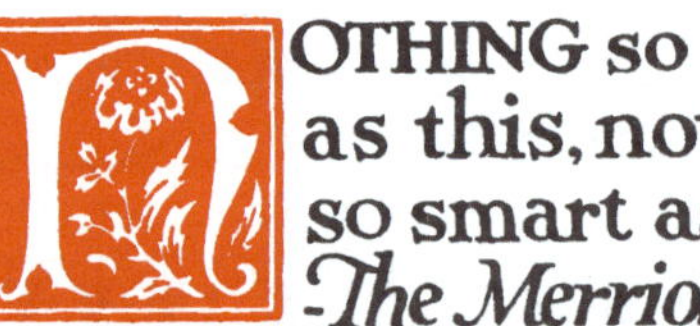OTHING so good as this, nothing so smart as this *-The Merrion C C* ~ for all 'round sports wear ~ Bilt primarily for the golfer, it thinks nothing of the tufest servis, yet it is eazful enuf & wel-bred enuf for any clubhouse veranda. Like all John Wards it bespeaks distinction

Mail orders shipt the day receivd. Send size and address on a postal A catalog, gladly ~

20th Century Limited

The accepted way of making the overnight journey between Chicago and New York

TRADE-MARKED LUMBER PRODUCTS

Now Include the Four Most Useful Building Woods

Douglas Fir
Cal. White Pine
Oak
Southern Pine

DELIGHT
in the New
WONDERLAND

a playground
~unique
~fascinating
~beautiful

When you buy your
railroad ticket, ask
for the ~
STOPOVER
in

WONDERLAND

Stay at least 3 days~
10 if you can ~ ~ ~
You'll enjoy every minute!

WS

West-

MICHIGAN

The

Playground of a Nation

Also the land-O-

water sports

Effects that Command!

It's up to the letter designer to attract the eye of the public.

In so doing he must create new effects in order to command the attention.

These few pages for examples

W

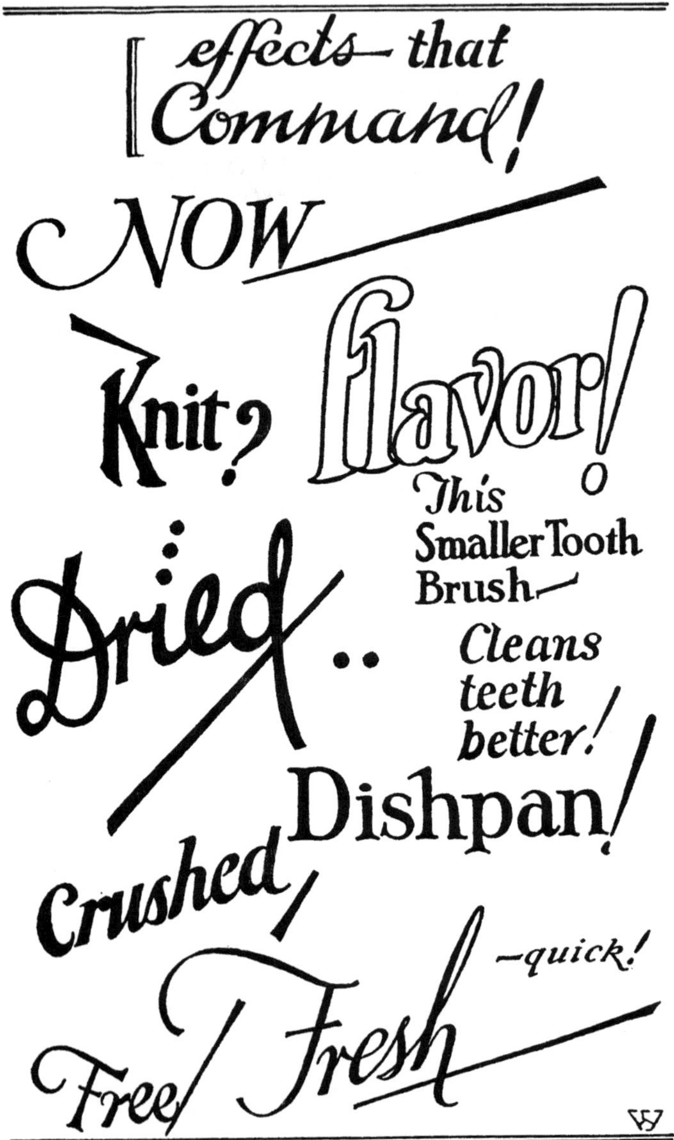
effects that Command!
NOW
Knit?
Flavor!
This Smaller Tooth Brush—
Dried..
Cleans teeth better!
Dishpan!
Crushed/
—quick!
Free/ Fresh
WS

Advertising

Bread
Iced
the Coolest
New
good Pacific
life
The
Splash
Clams
choice
New Delicious

Free Beautiful Now! Use & Are you letting your skin grow old?

The Before

23 New Models

fine Safety

Refined for Disks

Free! Lycoming

Genuine Now! Call for

my secret How?

that never fades

hour! fair!

Announcing–

Drink more milk If!

figures? "a sensible habit"

Speaks! Zero!

The Utility Coupe

!

The True Blue

ruined

for, real enjoyment

Keep fit

Ask for

Eat!

Steel Throughout

quality you can taste!

California

for Lunch

freckles "THE QUITTER"!

at

The

Where ever you go,

Restful

Lounge Car

Smart

but durable

the

Great!

best way

Springs

to begin

later

Which?

Fine

Radio

new *Southwest*

Fall *Gain!*

EVENT **efficiency**

bran ***Ask***

The

best

way

to

California

winter

mail this

New!

for you!

The New Vogue in Shirts

Classmates!
Beneficial and
"fresh"! California's finest
Will it be
the HOME
of your dreams?
Grated
mornin'!
Your
to enjoy!
The
exactly! The Charm

Pineapple Pie

Banish thirst The

THRILL YOU SO

Punctures repaired

Here is

It loads like

trimness

the pen

"None Better Obtainable at Any Price— Costs You Less"

Ready RealBoys

this-Danger!

Harvey

Springs

This is the Right way!

Pipe

Perfect

send for this catalog

The New

Free to You!

Object-

Take Advantage

VS

Whipped

Everyweek

Type Nine

Perfected

File! of Are

New With

Vital

Because

Prefer Unit

WY

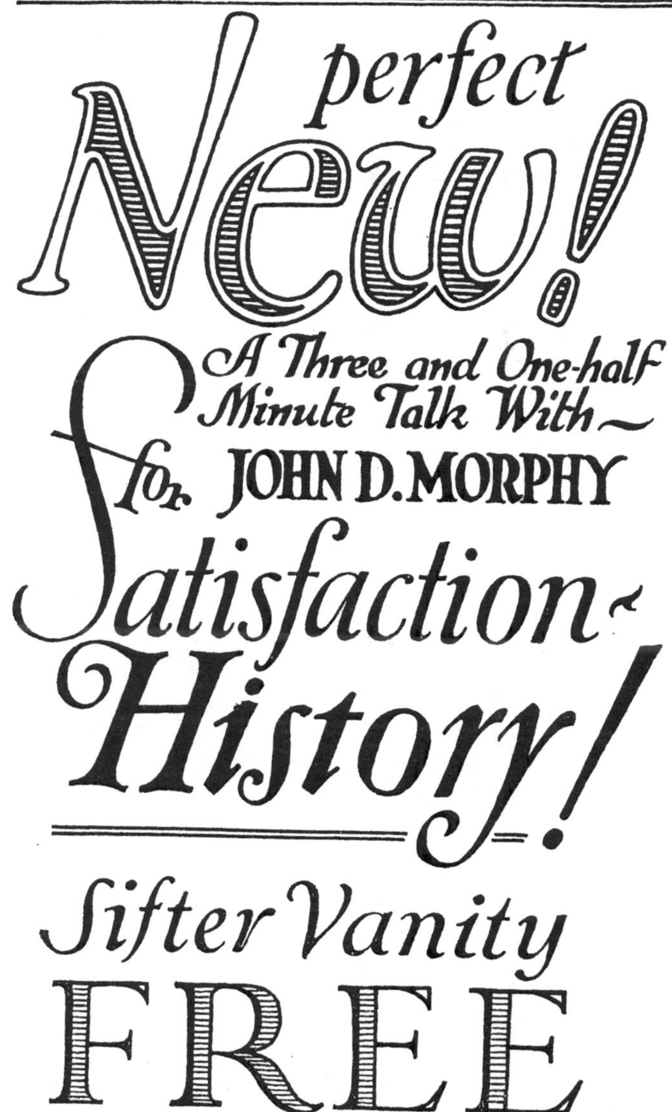
perfect
New!
A Three and One-half
Minute Talk With—
for JOHN D. MORPHY
Satisfaction-
History!
Sifter Vanity
FREE

Three Sale

3 for $1 Fall right

Men! For.

one

Furniture!

Matched

Nifty LOOK For
Flapper Styles STYLE
Take GUARANTEED
Unbeatable!
Two Great !
Sensational!
A Pretty Flat Million YEAR!
"Congratulations"
Specials!
Frocks for Flappers-

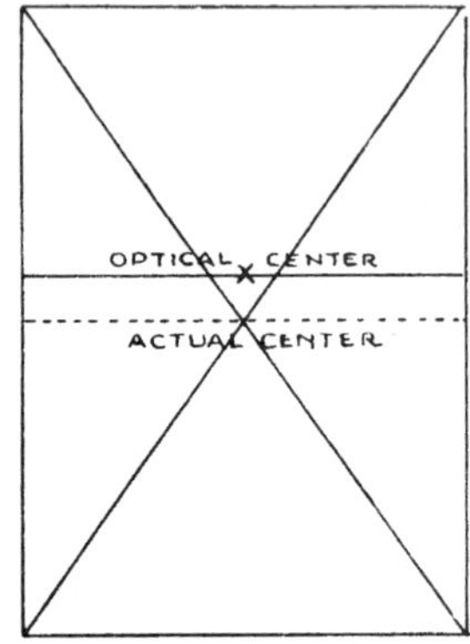

WHERE THE EYE STOPS

GENERAL LAW OF CENTER THE OPTICAL CENTER IS ABOVE CENTER. LAW IS THE REASON

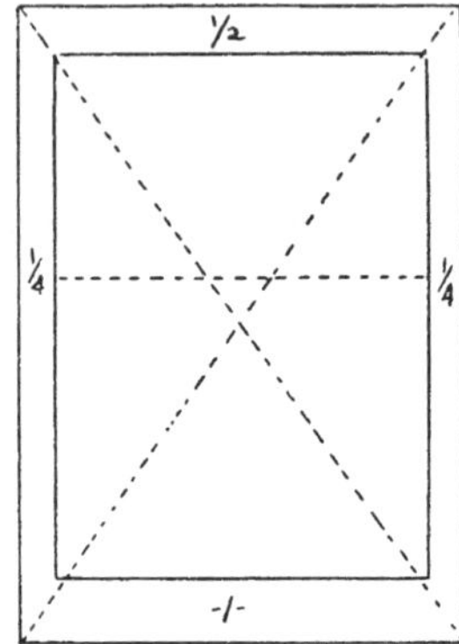

MOST PLEASING MARGIN

MARGIN- IS TO HAVE THE WIDEST AT THE BOTTOM THE TOP NEXT- THE SIDES ALIKE

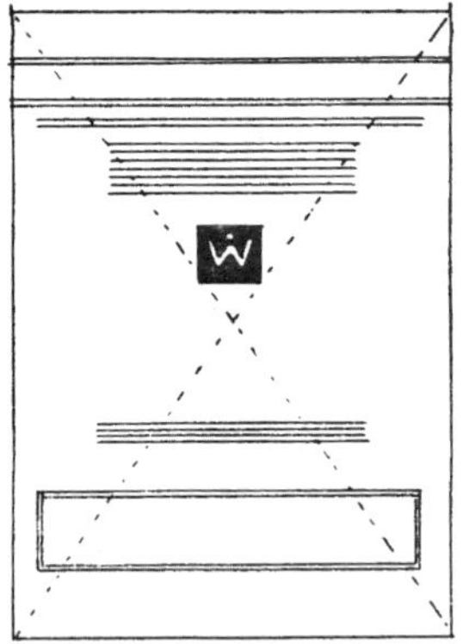

A PLACE FOR BLACK

ON THE OPTICAL CENTER IS A SPOT FOR SOLID BLACK OR A LITTLE TOUCH OF COLOR

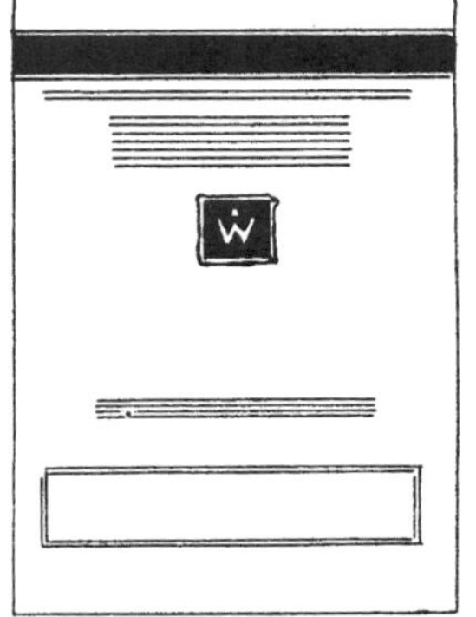

HEADING OF A PAGE

THE HEADING IS WHAT THEY WANT SEEN (FIRST) SO WE MAKE IT (BLACKER)

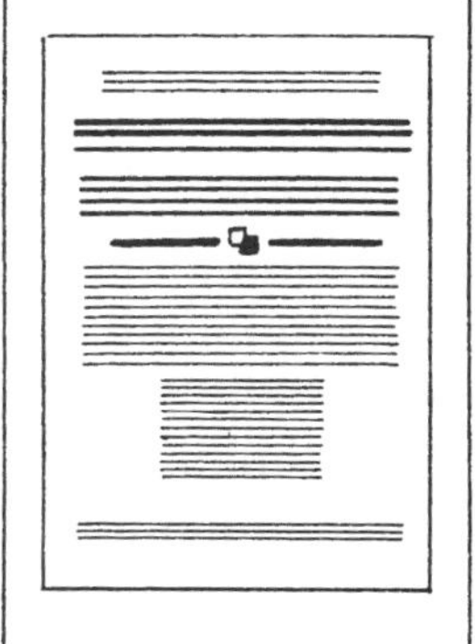

IN GOOD BALANCE

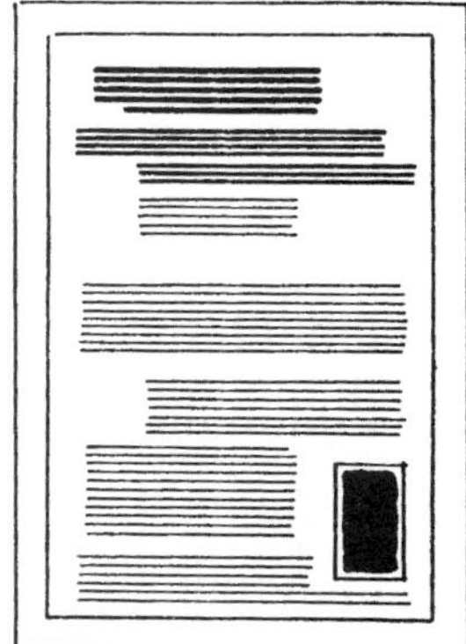

POORLY BALANCED

A BADLY BALANCED PAGE OF LETTERING FAILS PRIMARILY IN IT'S OBJECT BECAUSE IT DISTRESSES THE NERVE THROUGH THE SIGHT.

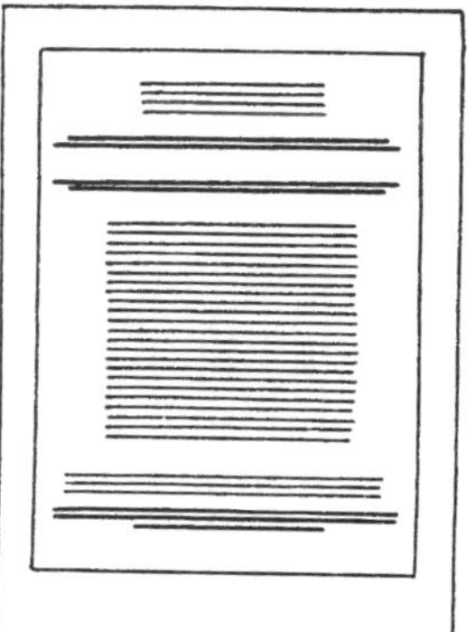

VERY GOOD BALANCE

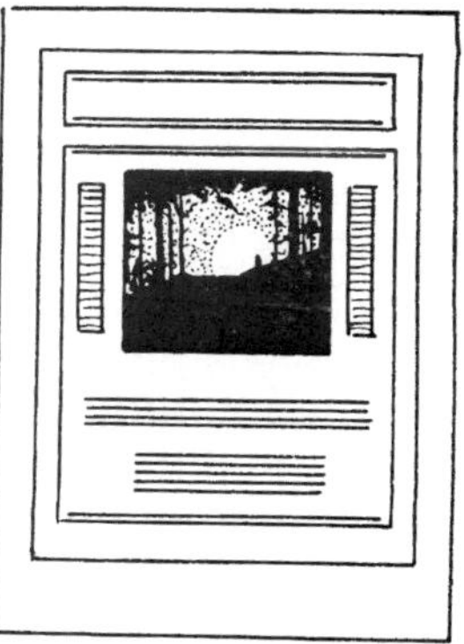

PICTURE BALANCE

IT PUTS THE EYE OF THE HUMAN BEING OUT OF LINE WITH THE LAW OF GRAVITATION — THE APPLICATION OF THE LAW OF GRAVITATION TO THE EYE IS CALLED BALANCE.

WY

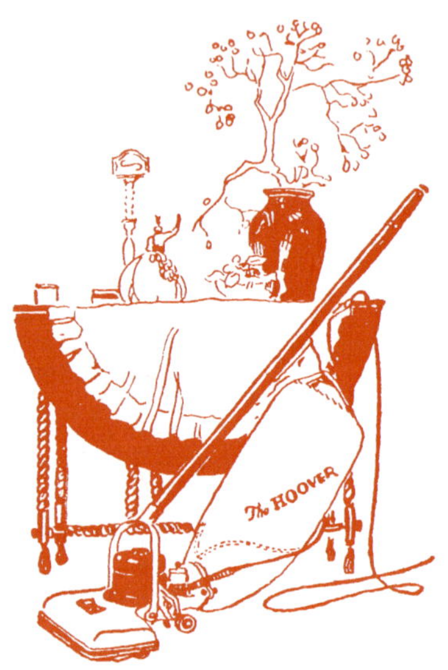

Rugs "like new" after 14 years

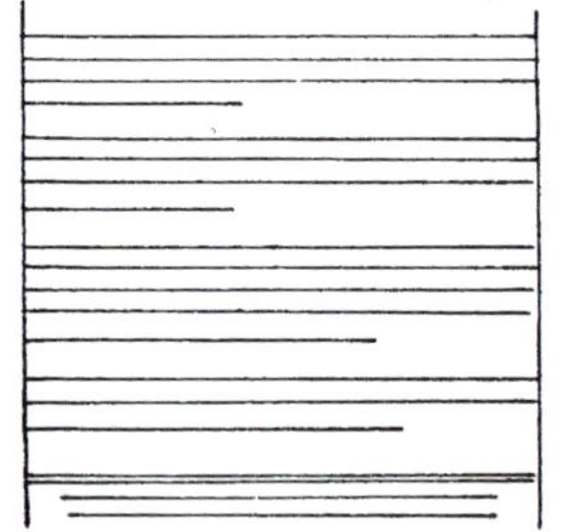

The HOOVER

Big Advertisers find pen technique an assent to the campaign. Drawings for Advertised products such as the Hoover Electric Cleaners. Take on New life because of Resourcefulness of Artists.

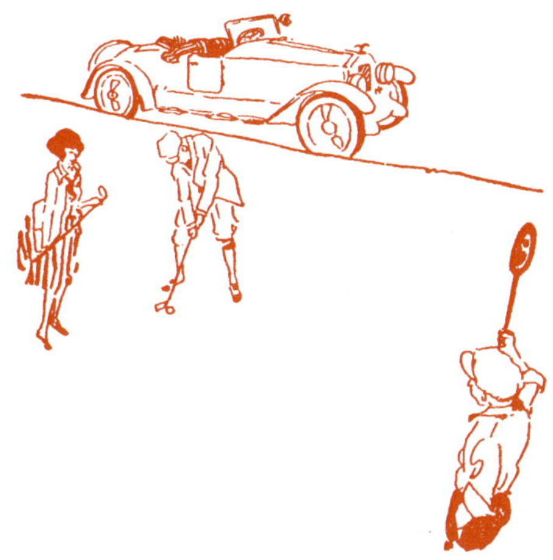

MASON CORDS

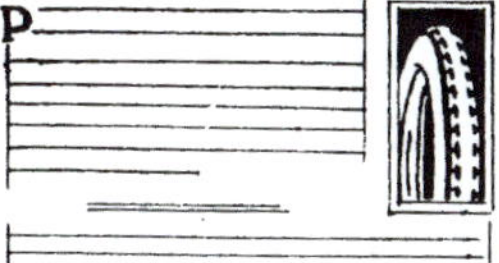

THIS ILLUSTRATION ATTRACTS BECAUSE OF THE ANGLE FROM WHICH THE DRAWING WAS MADE

Occasionally a series deliberately sets out to break these rules and do something new.
The results are interesting, and they do attract the attention.
The best recent example of it is found, perhaps, in a series of illustrations for Mason Cord tires.
The artist draws his compositions from an elevation. One is reproduced that is worthy of study. It shows a car drawn up at a curb line, a man and a woman in golf togs, and a cady, It is perhaps the perspective — view from a second-story window of a club house.
It is different and therefore compelling to a public accustomed to conventional compositions.

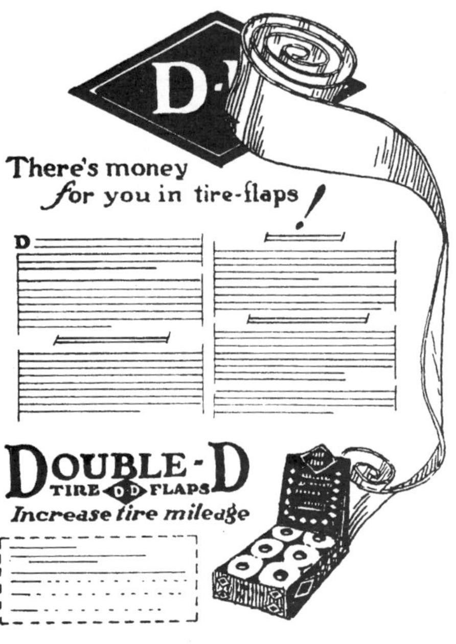

The purpose of this "LAYOUT" is to lead to the container and coupon

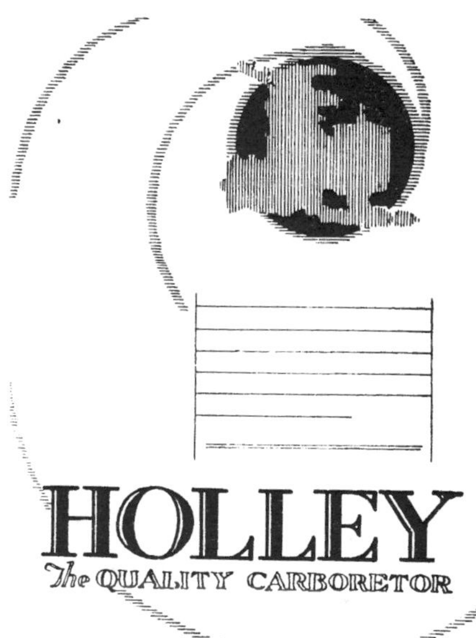

Two gray lines make the point to be emphasized the bull's-eye of the advertisement

W

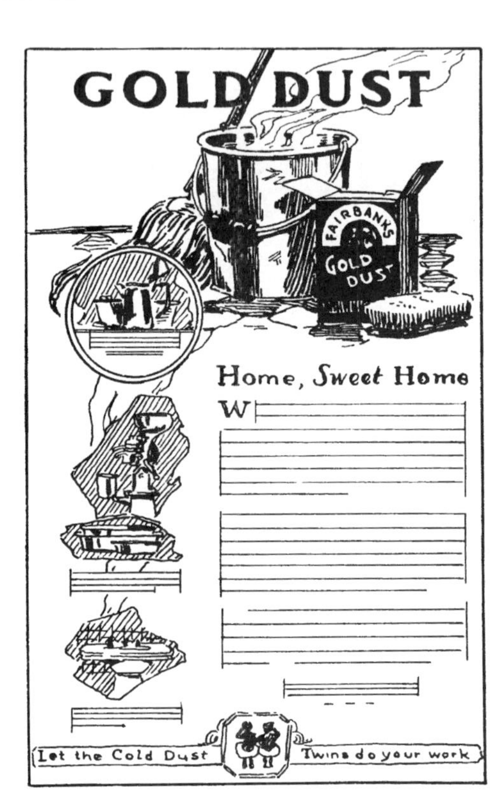
GOLD DUST
FAIRBANKS
GOLD DUST
Home, Sweet Home
W
Let the Cold Dust
Twins do your work

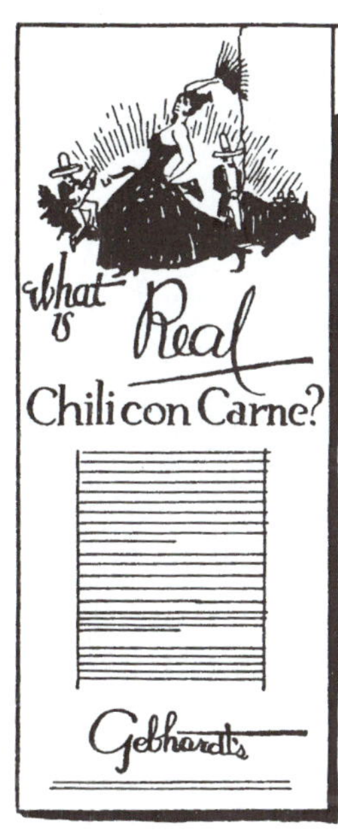
What is Real
Chili con Carne?
Gebhardt's

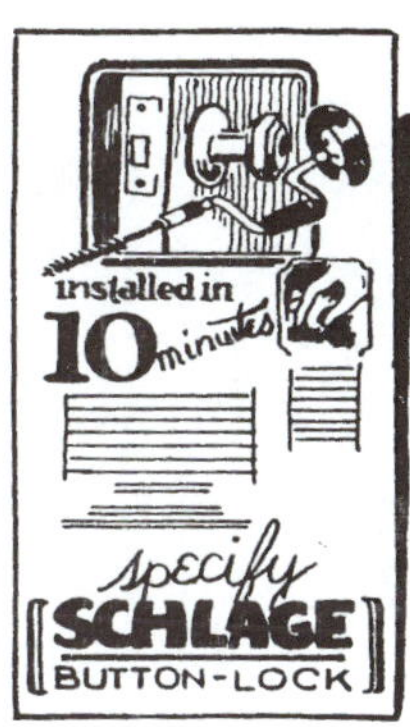
installed in
10 minutes
specify
SCHLAGE
BUTTON-LOCK

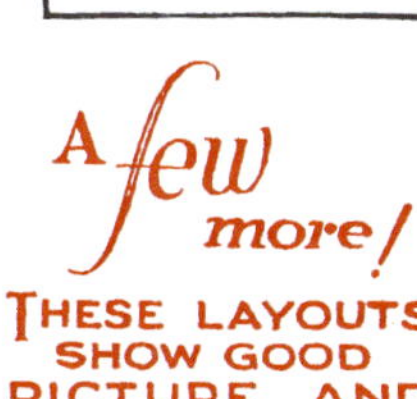
A few more!
THESE LAYOUTS
SHOW GOOD
PICTURE AND
COPY BALANCE

The WARM
BATH
ROOM
TOBIAS
gas
HEATER

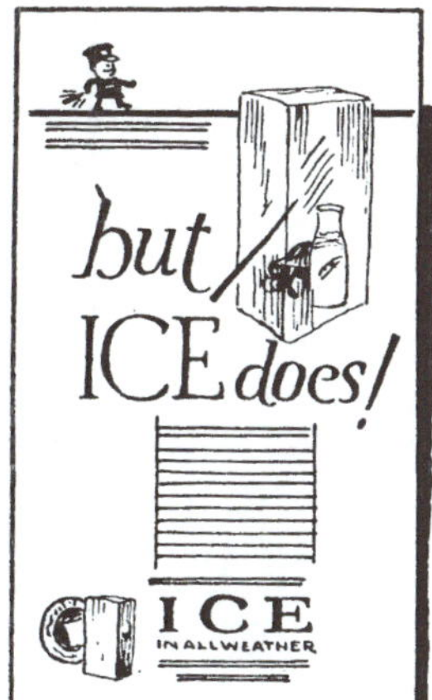
but
ICE does!
ICE
IN ALL WEATHER

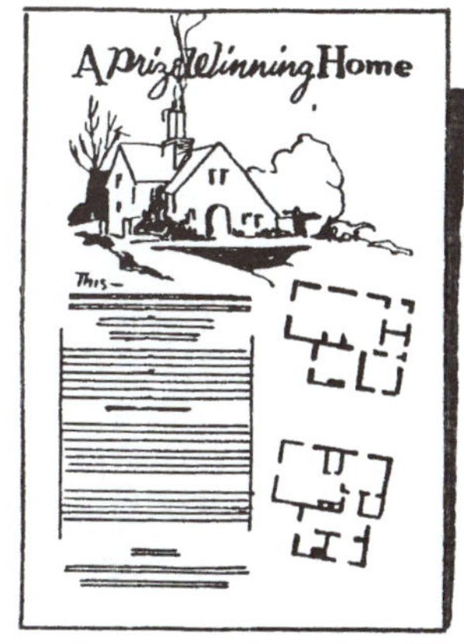
A Prize Winning Home
This—

"These also have "QUALITY"

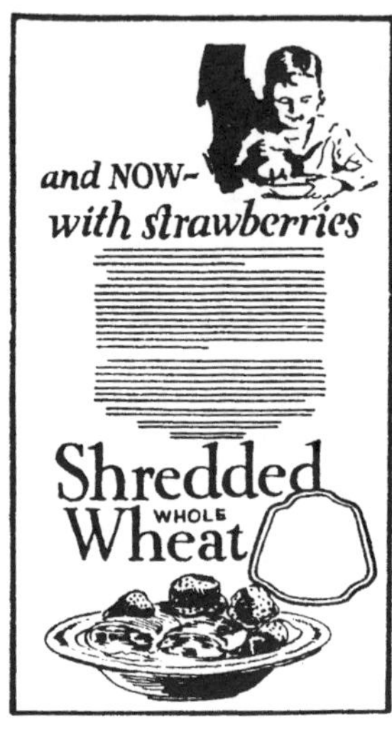

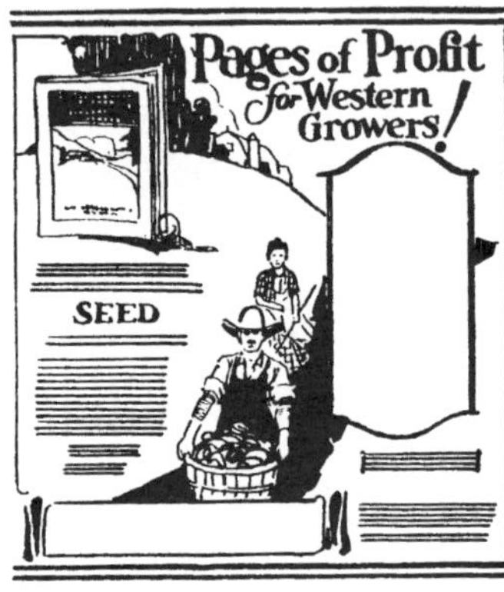

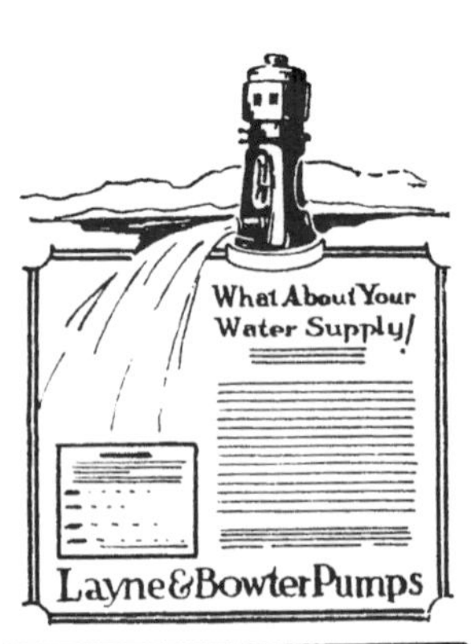

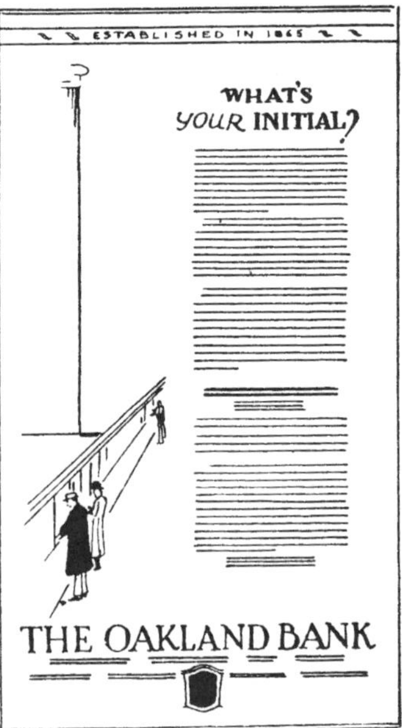

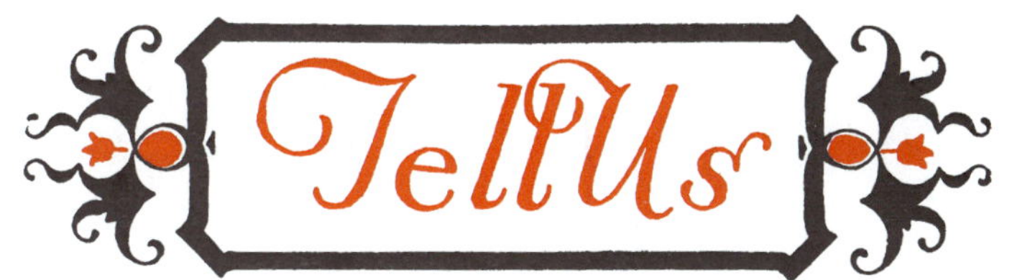

HOW
WHEN
WHY
and
WHERE
to use a
PANEL

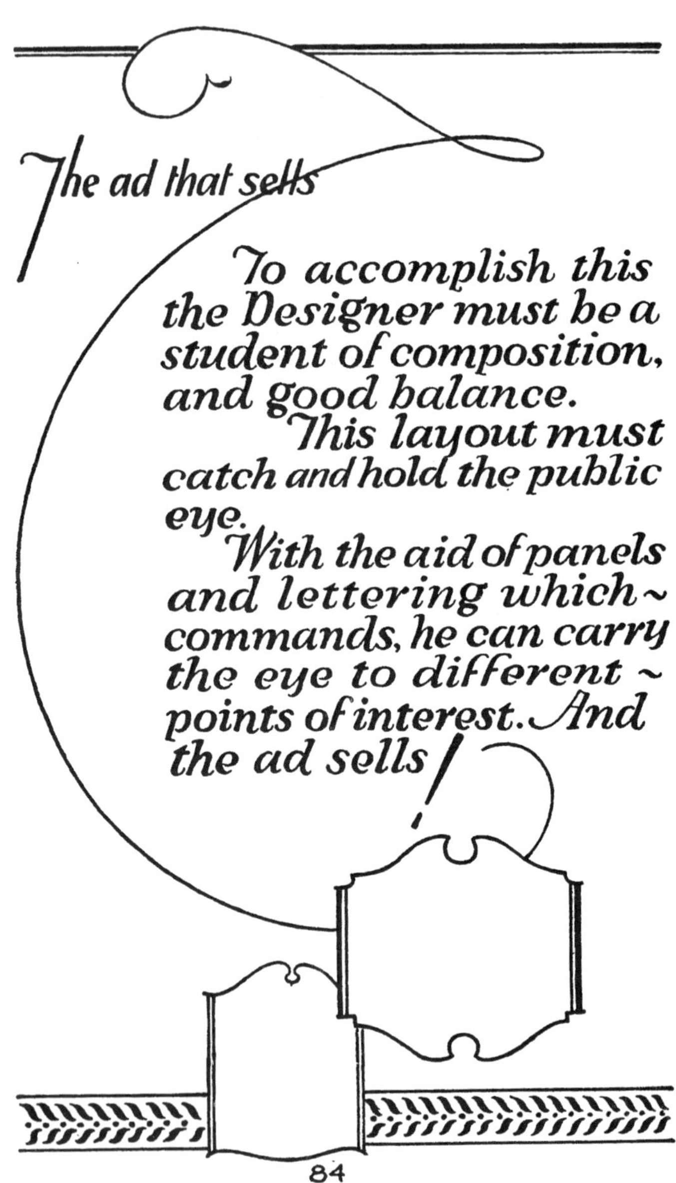
The ad that sells
To accomplish this
the Designer must be a
student of composition,
and good balance.
This layout must
catch and hold the public
eye.
With the aid of panels
and lettering which~
commands, he can carry
the eye to different ~
points of interest. And
the ad sells!

A LAYOUT DE-LUXE

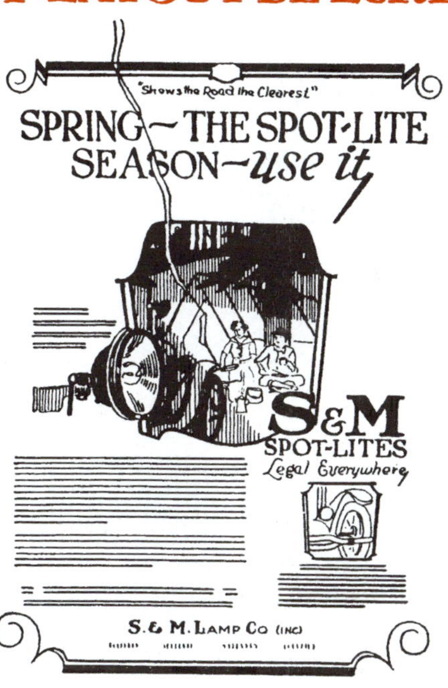

Panels have been of great value to obtain the *Balance and composition* in the above layout.

The smoke lines carry the vision through the Caption and on into the Picture, The Stop-Lite draws it into the copy. S&M being tied into the large Panel carry the vision on down with the aid of small Panel to trade-name. "Page Rules" also add to it

Whole Panels

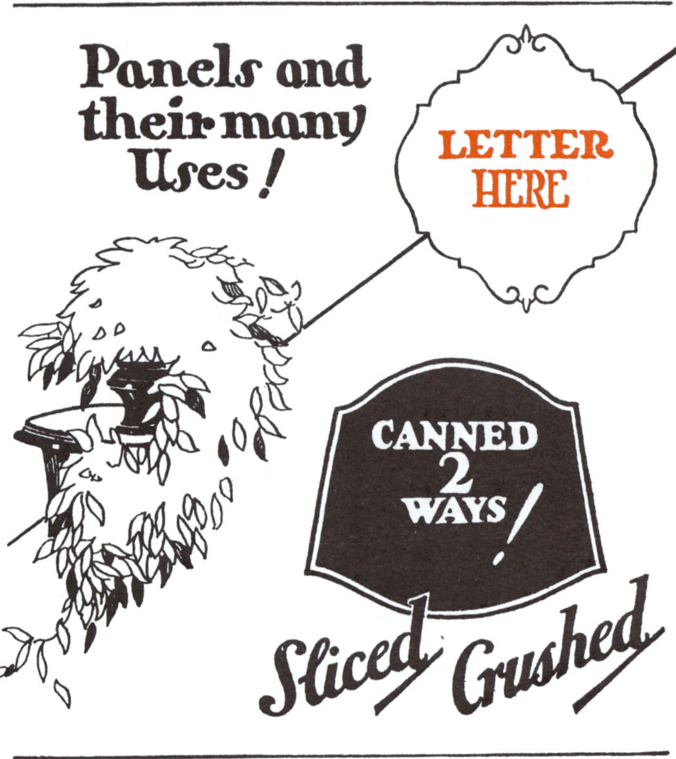

Panels are very helpful in getting good Balance to Layouts

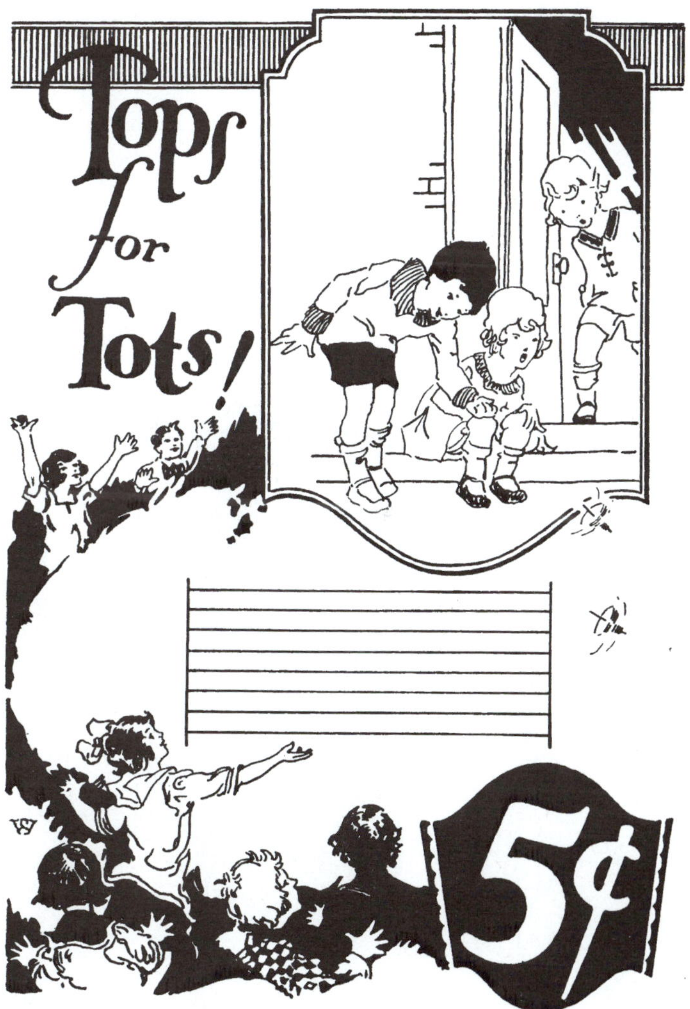
Tops for Tots!
5¢

Panels

PANELS ~ ~

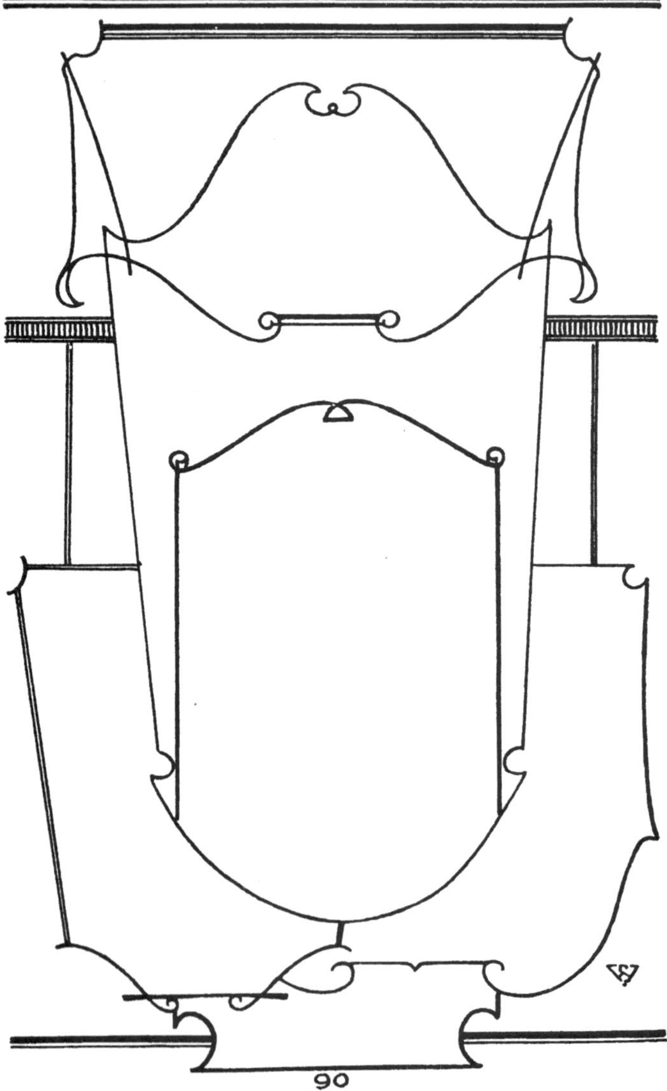

PANELS

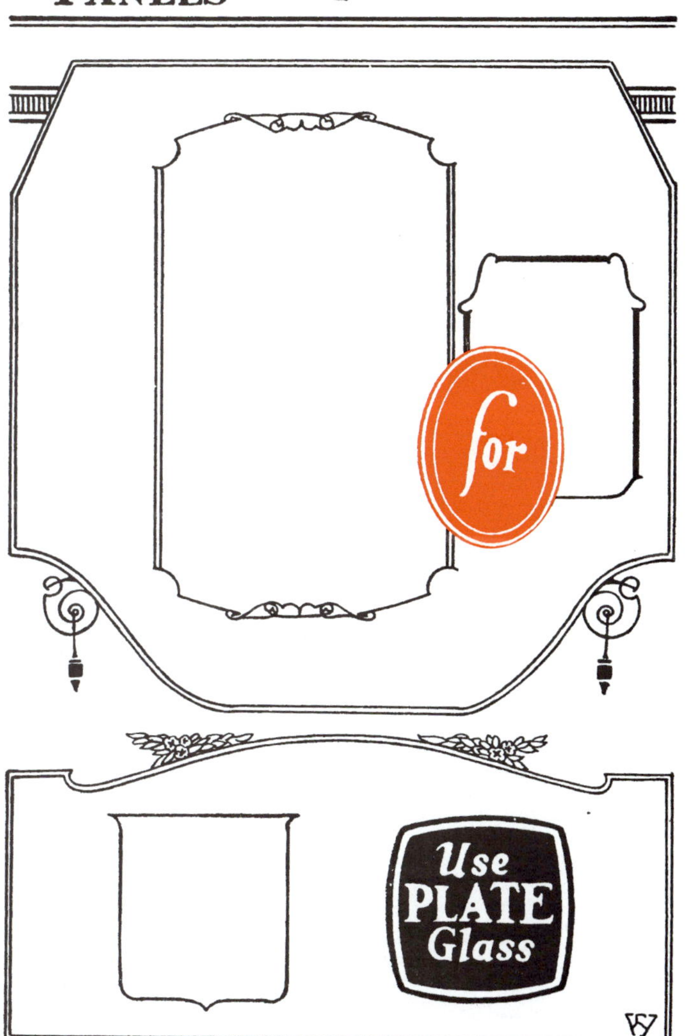

Panels

Panels

Half Panels // //

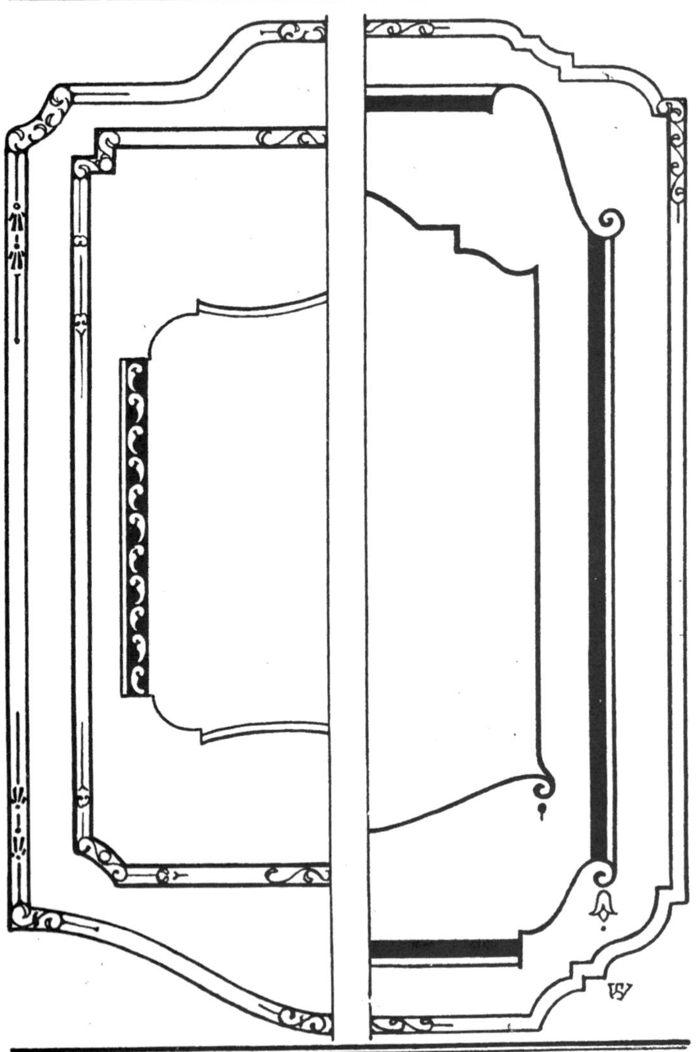

Half Panels

BOX CORNERS

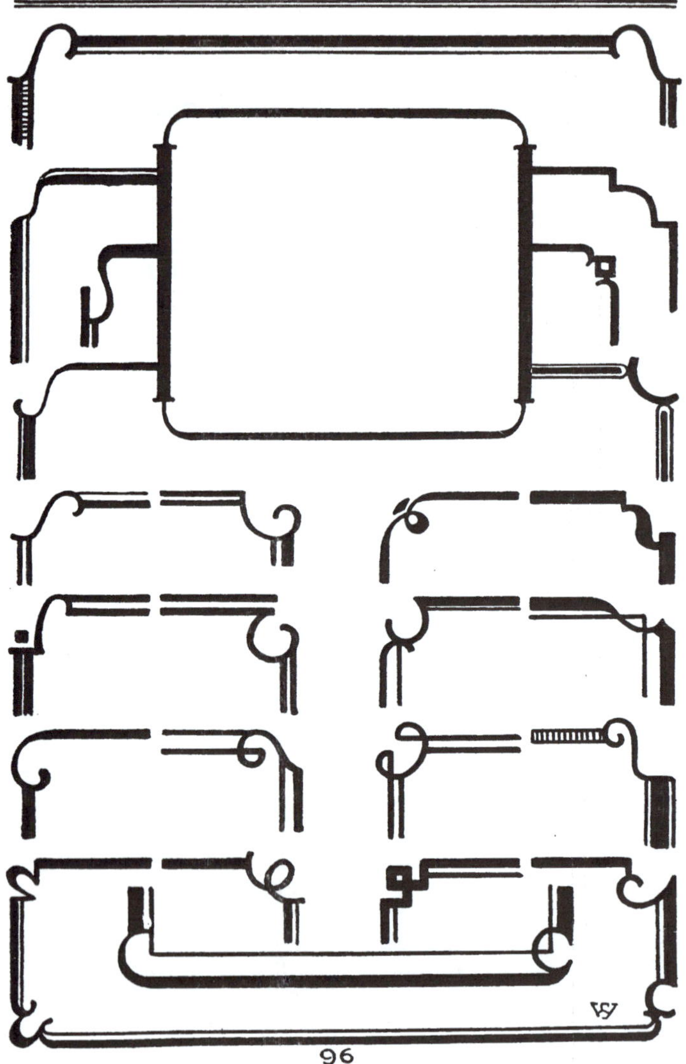

Page Rules

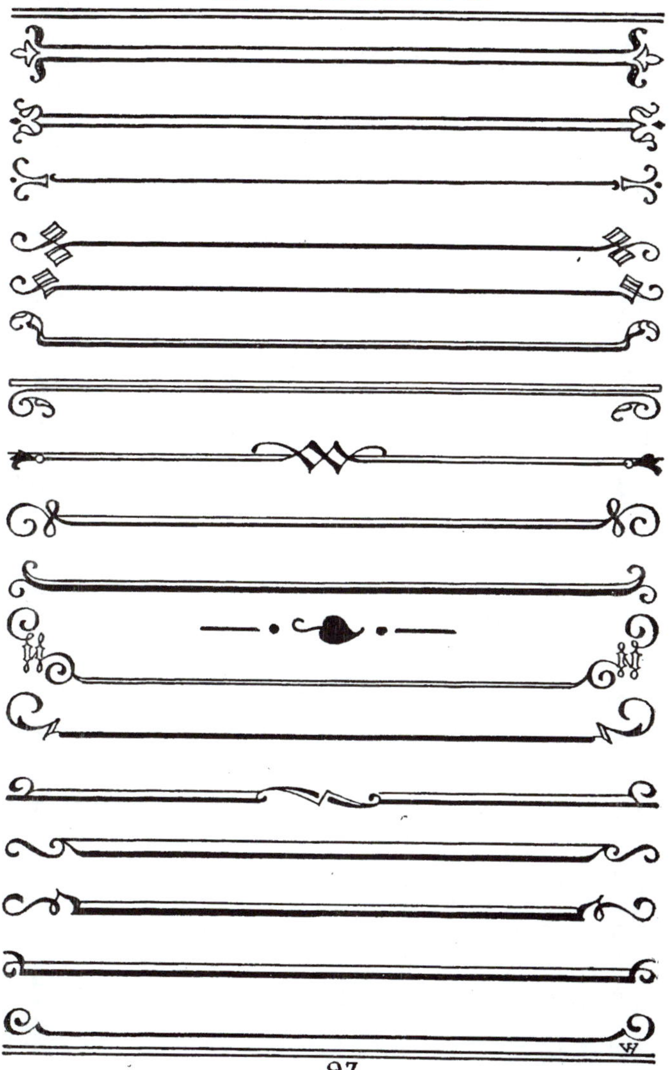

Page Rulers

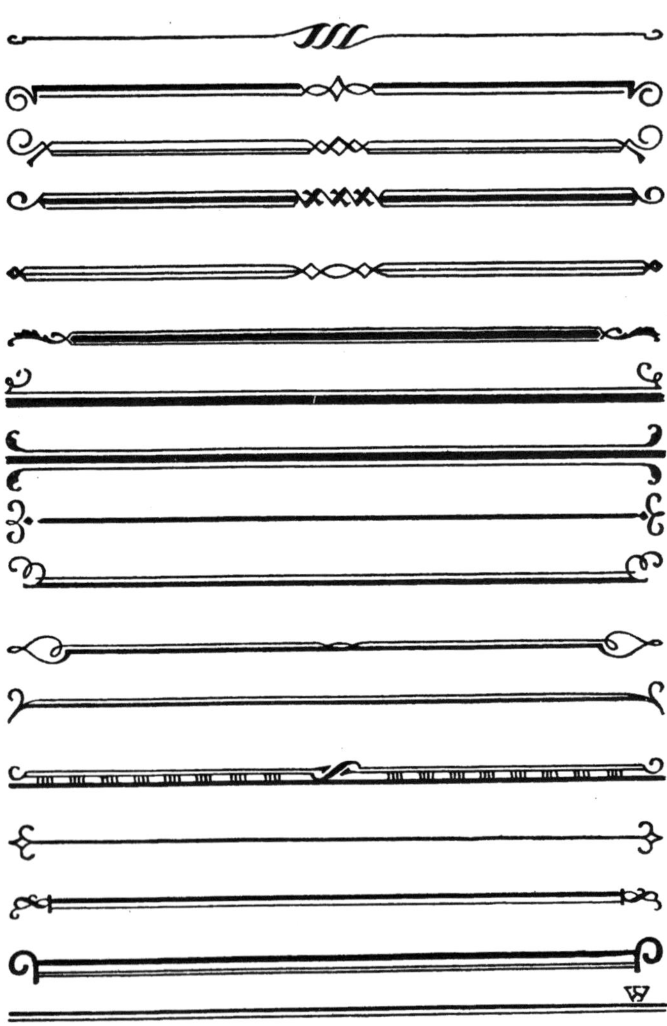

Border Suggestions

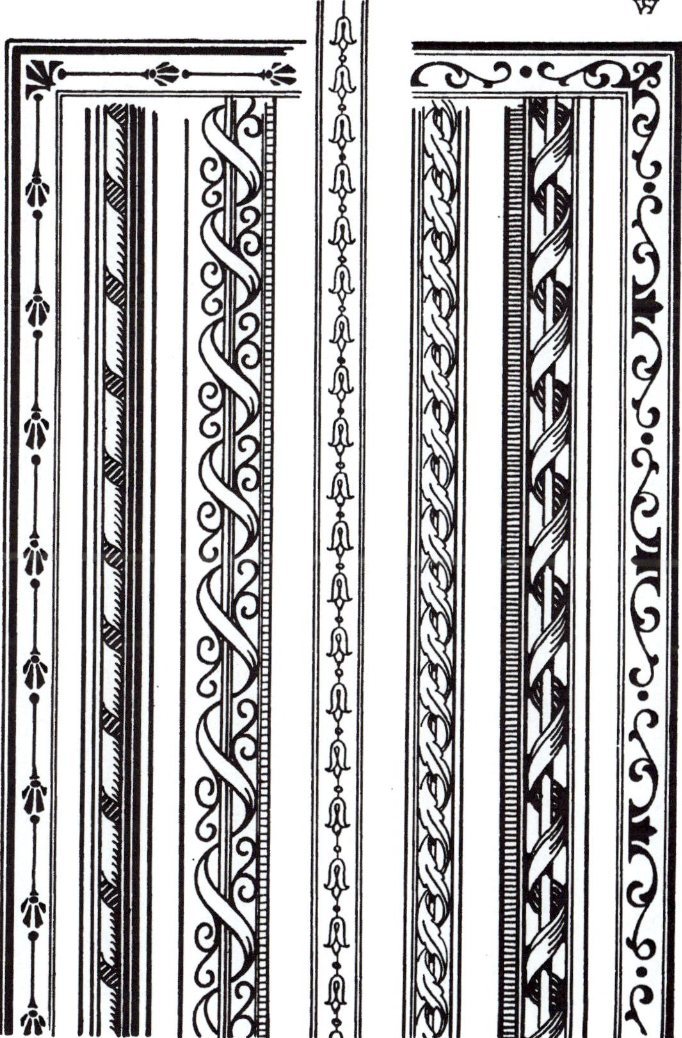

Border Suggestions

Border Suggestions

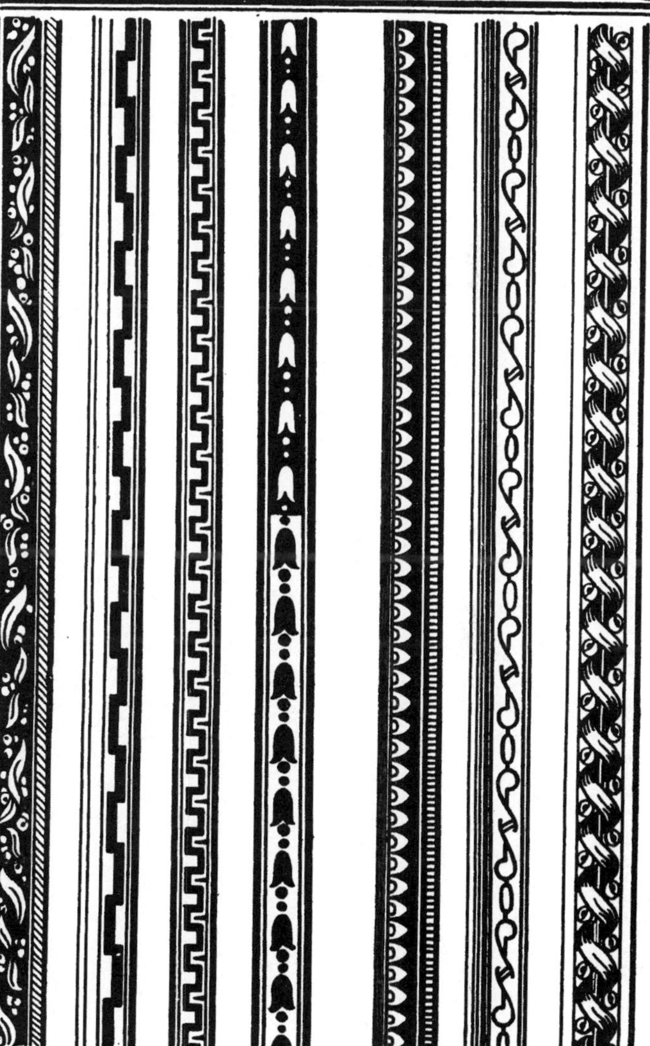

Border Suggestions

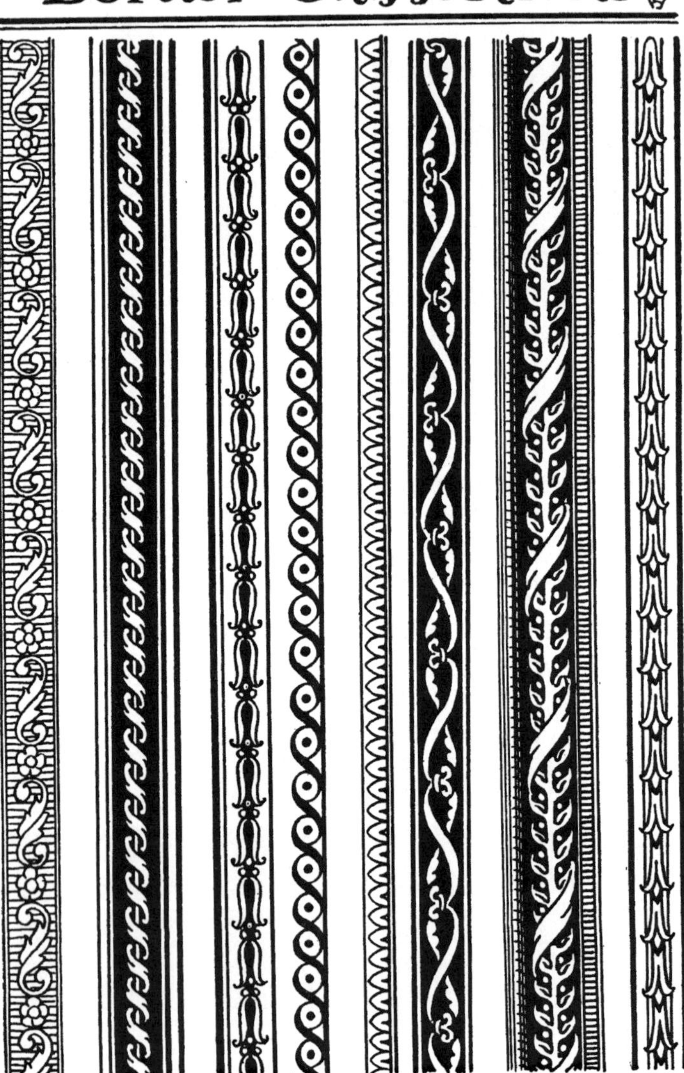

Border Suggestions

BORDER SUGGESTIONS

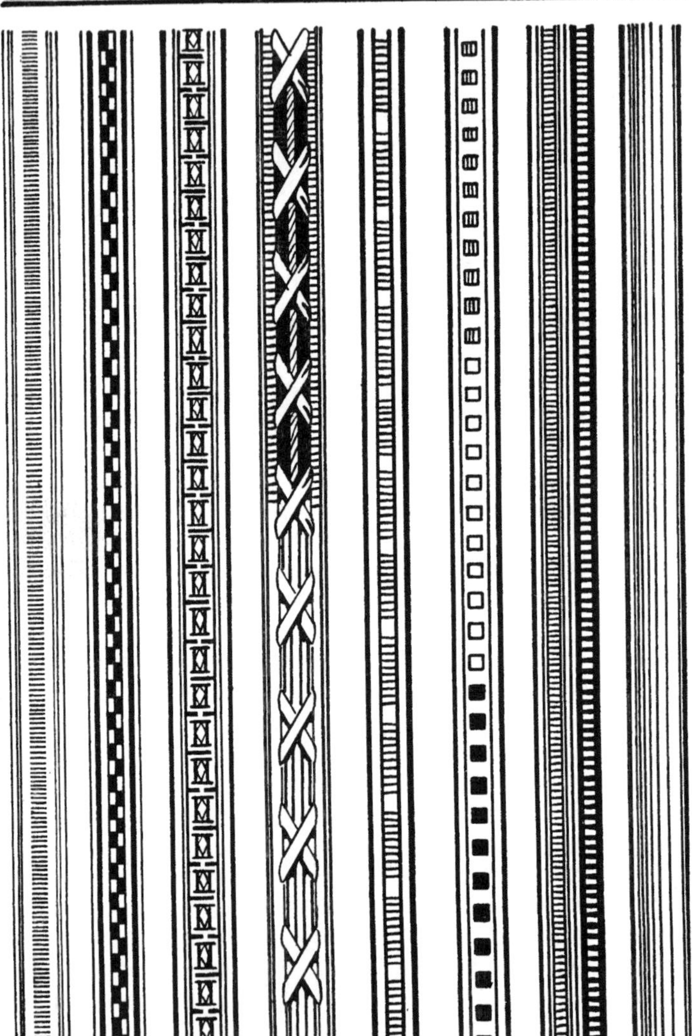

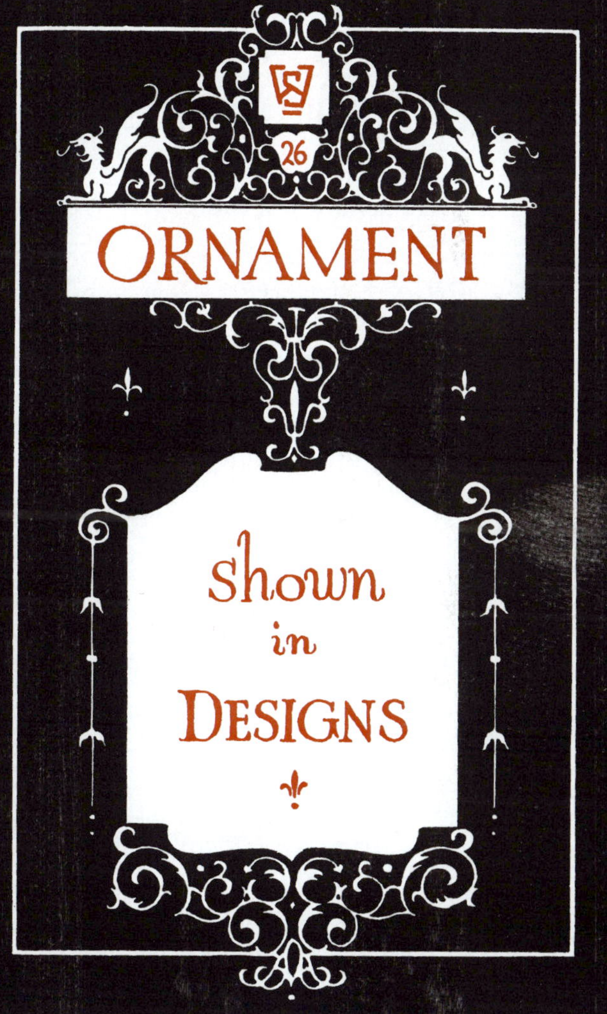

26
ORNAMENT
shown
in
DESIGNS

ORNAMENT

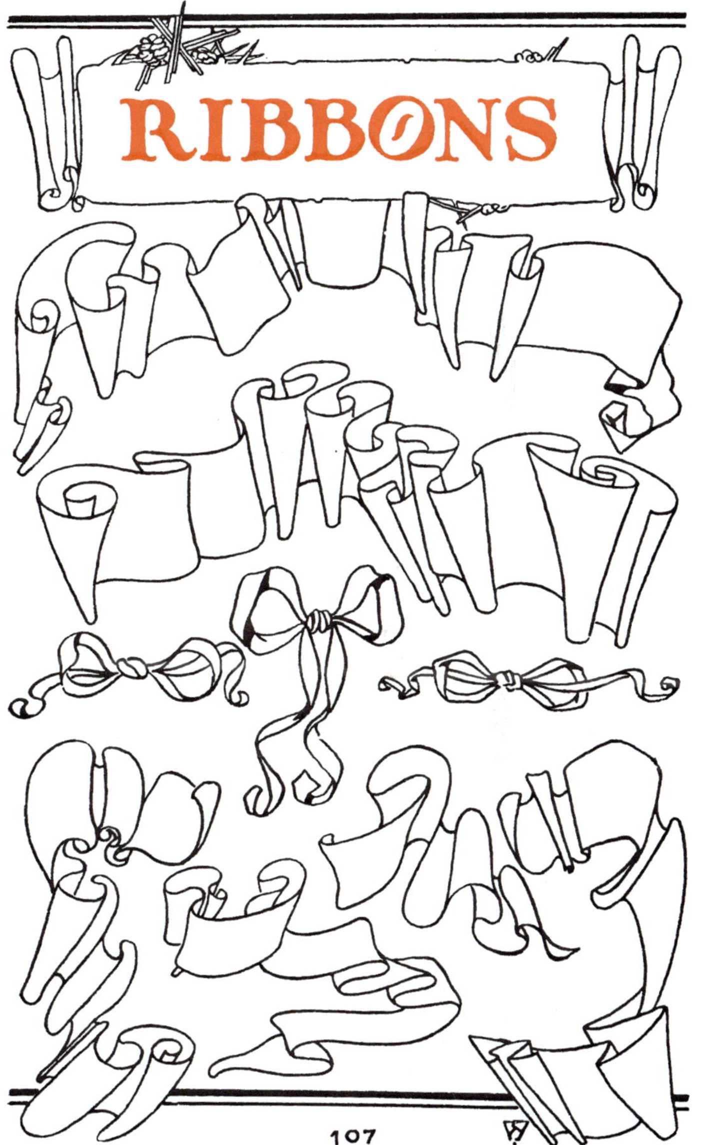
RIBBONS

Ribbons

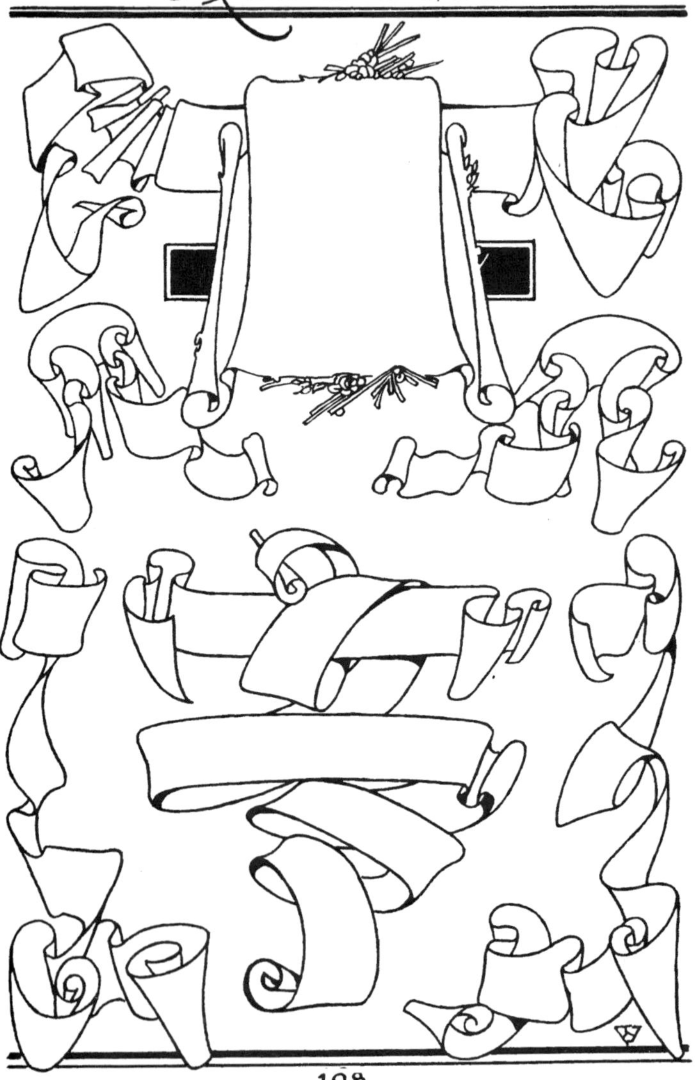

DINGBATS

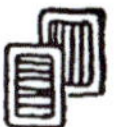

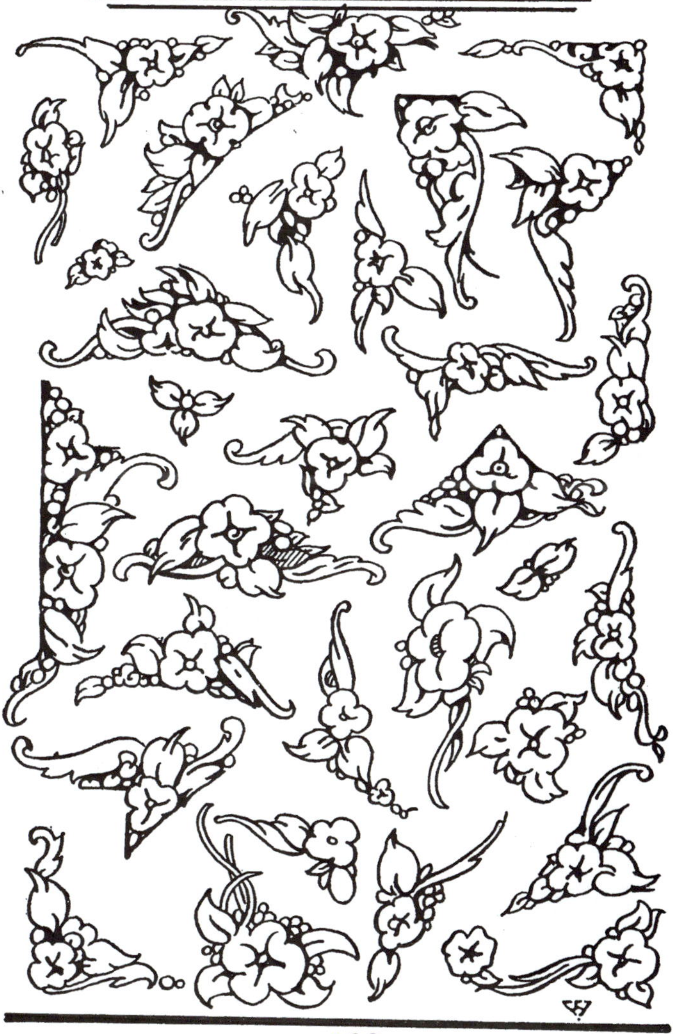

DINGBATS

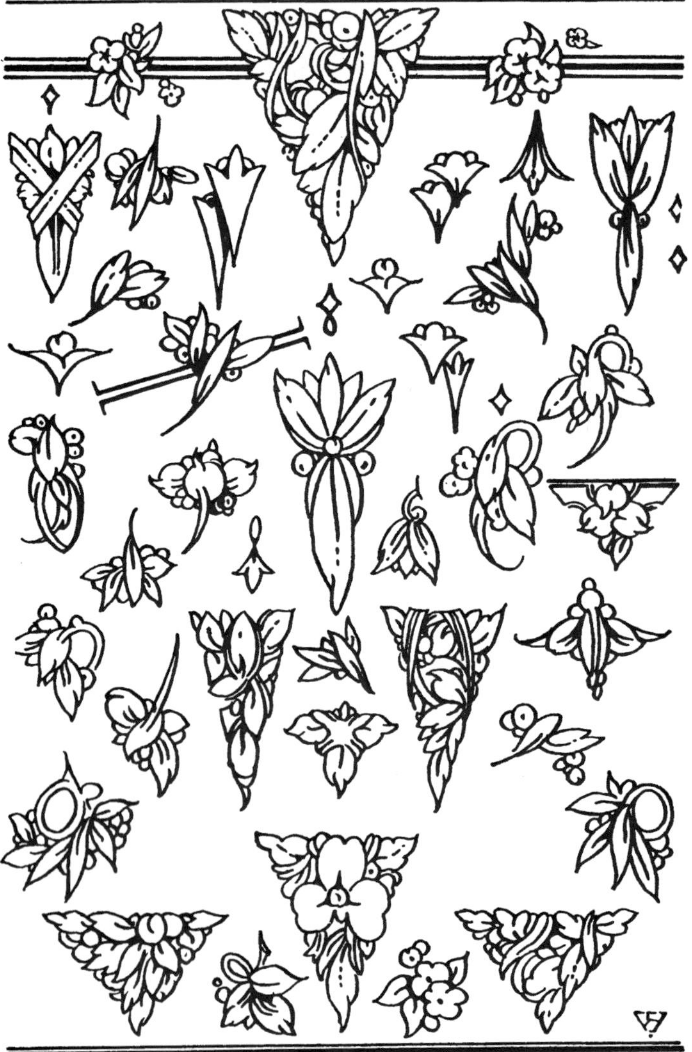

DINGBATS

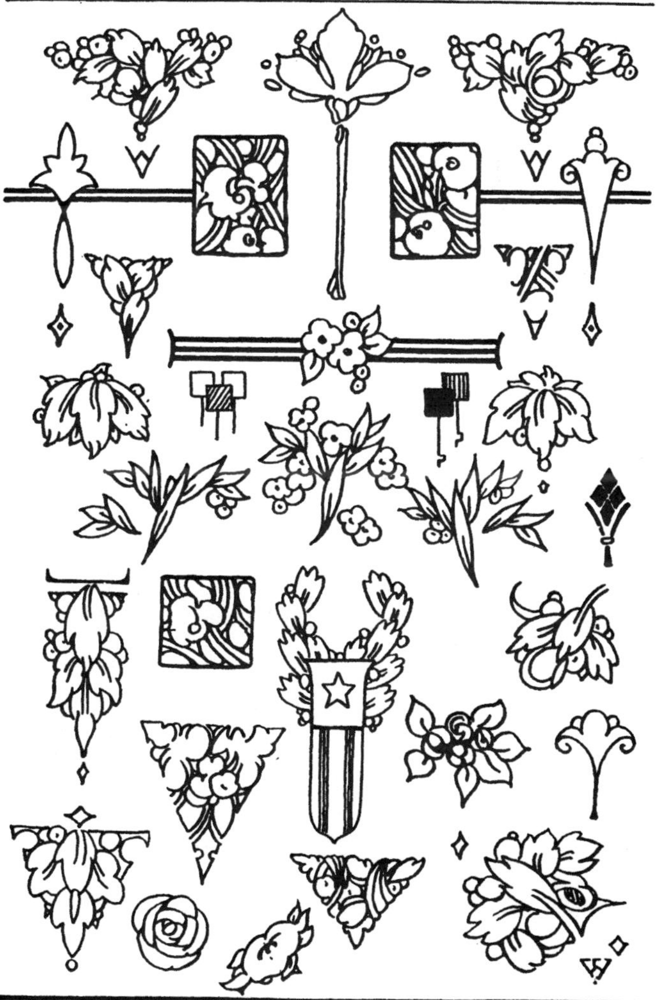

Dingbats

DINGBATS

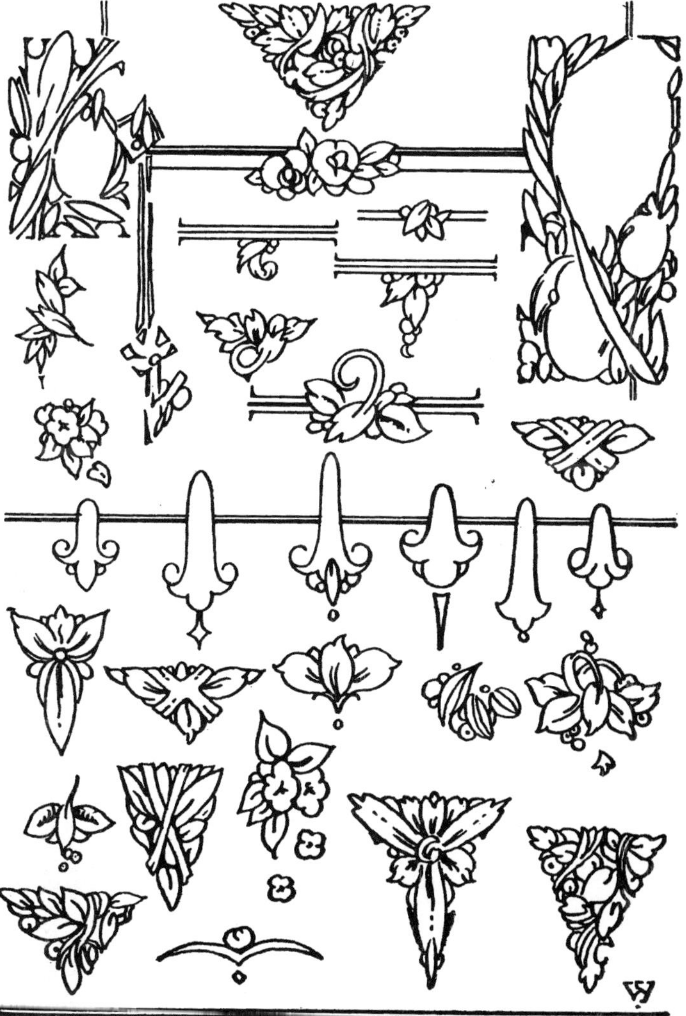

MASKS

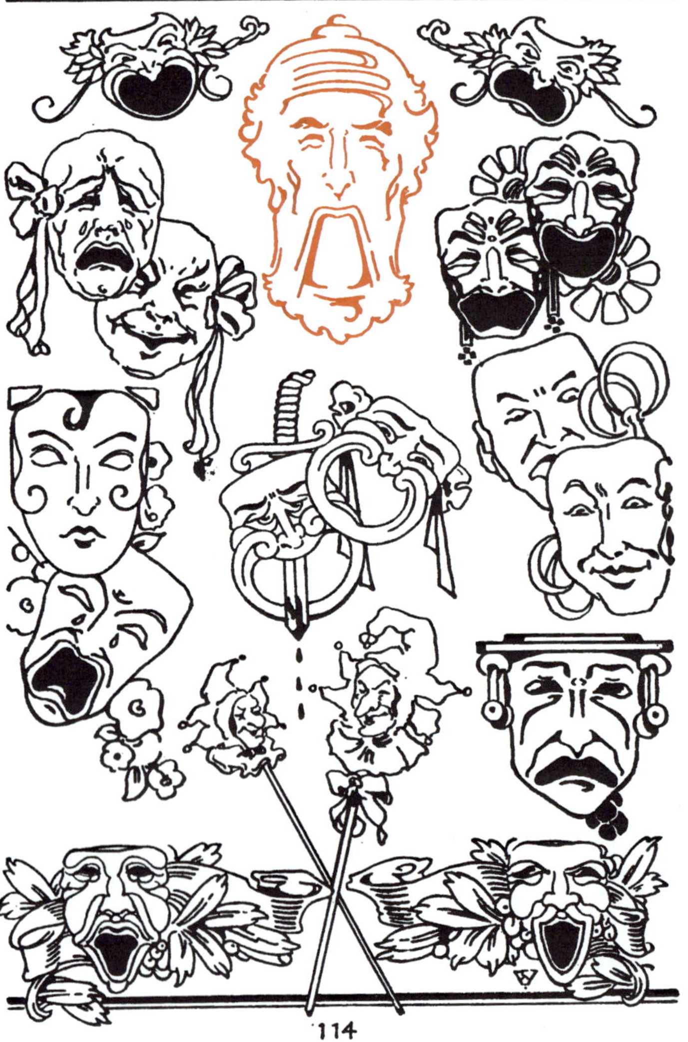

The Printers Rule

He measures ··· *up and down*
His width is · *one or more columns*
His height is in · *Points, Picas, Ems and Agate lines* ···············

There are	72	Points	to the	*inch*
" " "	12	" "	"	a *pica*
" " "	6	Picas	"	the *inch*
" " "	6	Ems	"	" "
" " "	12	Picas	"	" *col.*
" " "	14	Agate lines	"	" *inch*

one Agate equals 5½ points ····

He finds the number of lines of *type* to the inch, by dividing 72 by the *type size* in points. "*Example*," (8 *point type used*) (72) divided by (8) equals (9) lines Type sizes run from 3½ points to 72 points high. ············

One column newspaper is 12 picas or (2) inches wide, ·· Magazine columns are more

"*Example*" Copy space 4 columns wide - 140 lines deep, ~ equals a spaee 8x10 inches, When type size is not mentioned ~ ~ ~

Point Faces

1 POINT

2 POINTS

3 POINTS

4 POINTS

6 POINTS

8 POINTS

12 POINTS

14 POINTS

18 POINTS

24 POINTS

AND 30-36-42-48-60-72-POINT FACE TYPE

Most used Type Characters

THESE ARE 48 POINT TYPE FACE

Artcraft ~ ~ ~

Caslon Bol -

Cheltenham -

Cooper ~ ~ ~

Cooper Bl

Goudy Bold

Goudy Italic

Parsons ~ ~ ~

Caslon Ital.

Publication Sizes

Publication	Page Size
American Magazine	7 x 10 3/16
Good Housekeeping	" "
The Literary Digest	7¼ x 10 13/16
Life ~ ~ ~ ~ ~	8 x 10
Country Life	8¼ x 12
Motor ~ ~	" "
House and Garden	8 5/16 x 11¼
Vanity Fair ~ ~	" "
Vogue ~ ~ ~	" "
Motor Life ~ ~	8 5/16 x 11 5/16
Saturday Evening Post	9⅜ x 12⅛
Ladies Home Journal	" "
Country Gentleman	" "
Womans Home Companion	" "
Newspaper ~ ~	17 x 21½
24 Sheet Billboard	11x25 feet

Sketches drawn ~ inch to the foot

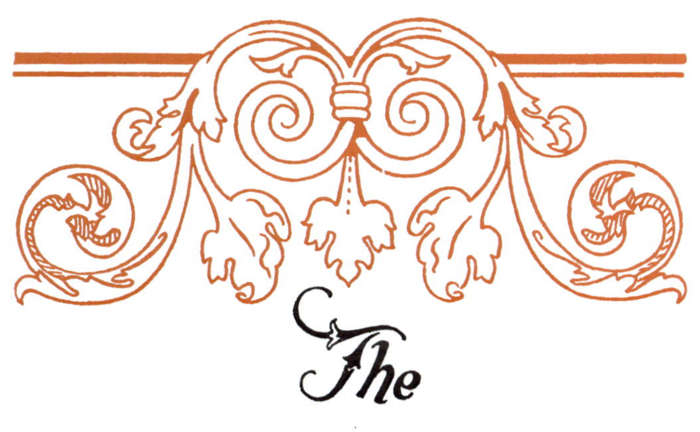

The ROMAN LETTER

The letters themselves are a development from the Arabic and Greek, and later, the Roman. The letter we call Roman is the most beautiful in existence, and forms the basis for nearly all civilized alphabets. It reached a very high development in inscriptions on tombs and monuments in ancient and mediaeval Rome and Italy. It has been adapted and modified by nearly every type founder or letterer.

The Roman letter used in the English speaking nations has come down to us through the Italians and through the Germans it has grown into the modern German-Gothic, a letter which is very strong and heavy and solid, but lacking in grace or elegance.

The different national temperaments are well expressed in the type of lettering each uses. The graceful, light, and vivacious script came from France.

Roman has been brought to its highest modern development by the Englishman Wm. Caslon, and the heavy blackface type is distinctly German. W.

The Roman Letter

Is the most difficult to compose into words artistically, spacing of the letter plays a great share in the results.

Even color in lettering is obtained by keeping as near the same area of white between each letter as possible.

Letters may be widened or condensed to help fill the awkward hole.

OLD ROMAN

The letters on this plate were drawn from a photograph of a portion of the inscription at the base of the "Trajan Column" of Rome, dated (114 A.D.)

ABCDE
FGILM
NOPRS
T·QV·X

ROMAN

This alphabet of Capitals founded on the letters of the inscription on the base of Trajan's Column, Rome, erected between 106 and 110 A.D. The characters not given in the inscription are supplied, together with the Æ, Œ, and &.

This alphabet, though following the Trajan letters closely, has many points of variance. There is more difference in the proportion of the thick and thin strokes than in the original.

ABCDEF
GHIJKL
MNOPR
STUVW
XY-ÆŒ&

WY

ROMAN

These Capitals are based on the inscription on the monument of the Emperor Henry VII (Henry of Luxembourg) in Campo Santo, Pisa by Tino di Camaino, a pupil of Giovanni Pisano, dated 1315. Many of the letters of this inscription are superior in form to those of the Trajan inscription. The round letters are fuller and more smoothly rounded

ABCDEF
GHIIJKL
MMNOP
RSTUV-
XYZW

WY

ROMAN

These Capitals made for this special alphabet careful parallel studies of the types of Joannes Spira and Nicolas Jenson from the editions of Pliny, printed at Venice, That of Spira in 1469, Jenson's in 1476, And from Cicero's Epistles, printed by Jenson in 1470. The letters as they appear are the best of the assays, and are, different in detail from any existing type.

ABCDEF
GHIJKL
MMNOP
RSTUV
& Œ

GOTHIC

We find this capital a valuable one in the designing of monograms and ciphers; for title, motto, or inscription.

The general proportion of the letter is that of many of the illuminated initials found in manuscripts of the fifteenth century. The base of this alphabet comes from the *Champfleury* of Geofroy Tory, printed at Paris in 1529.

A B C D E

F G H J K

I L M N O

P R S T T

U V W W

X Y Z &

Old English

ABCDEF

GHIJKL

MNOPQ

RSTUW

XYZ&V?

abcdefghijkl

mnopqrstu

vwxyz1234

OLD ENGLISH

A B C D E F G

H I K L M N O

P Q R S T U V

W X Y Z abcdef

ghijklmnopqrstuv

wxyz1234567890

ABCDEFGH

IJKLMNOPQ

RSTUWYZX

Modern English

A B C D E

F G H I J

K L M N

O Q P R S

T U V W Y

a b c d e f g h i k

m p r s t u v w y

German Black Letter.

A B C D E F
G H I J K L
M N O P Q R
S T U V W
X Y Z

german black-
letter treated
freely-
abcdefghijkl
mnopqrstu-
vwxyz

Modern

A B C D E

F G H I J

K L M N

O P R S

T V W Y

A-Blackletter

A B C D E

F G H I J

K L M N

O P Q R S

T U V W X

Y Z

Lowercases

abcdefghik
lmnopqrst
uvwxyz "

abcdefghj
klmnopqrs
tuvwxy "

French Script

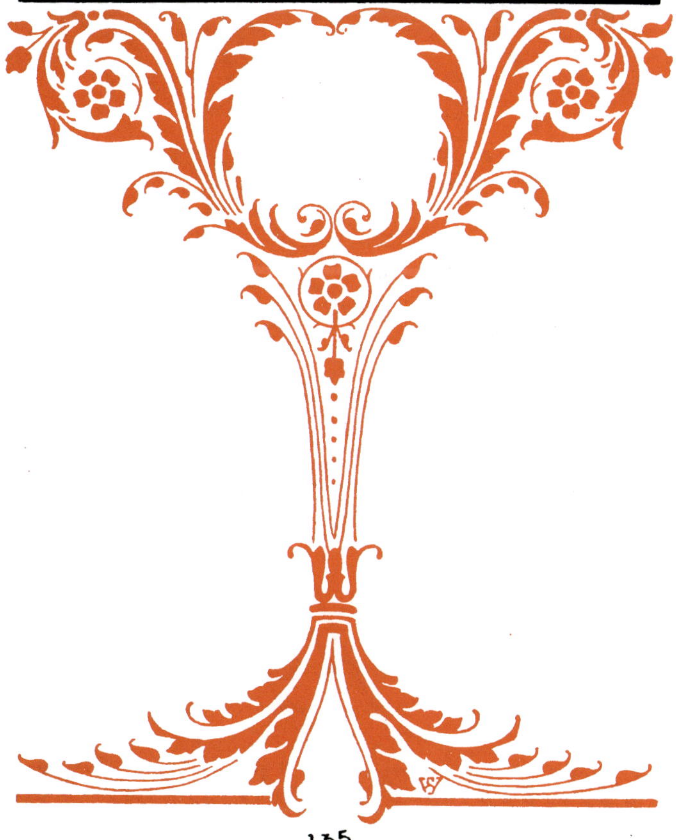

A B C D E

F F G H I

J K L M N

O P Q R S

T U V W X

Y Z & Th

abcdefighijkl

mnorrstupvwx

A B C D E

F G H I J

K L M N

O P Q R

S T U V E

W X Y Z

abcdefghijklmn

opqrstuvwxyz etc

A B C D

E F G H f

I K L N

M N Q R

S U V W

X Y Z &

ab eknrstw

ABCDEF

GHIJKL

MNOPQ

RSTUW

VXYZ&

abcdefghijk

lmnopqrst

uvwxyzz

slight script–

A B C D

E F G H

I J K L

M O P Q

R S T U

V W X Y

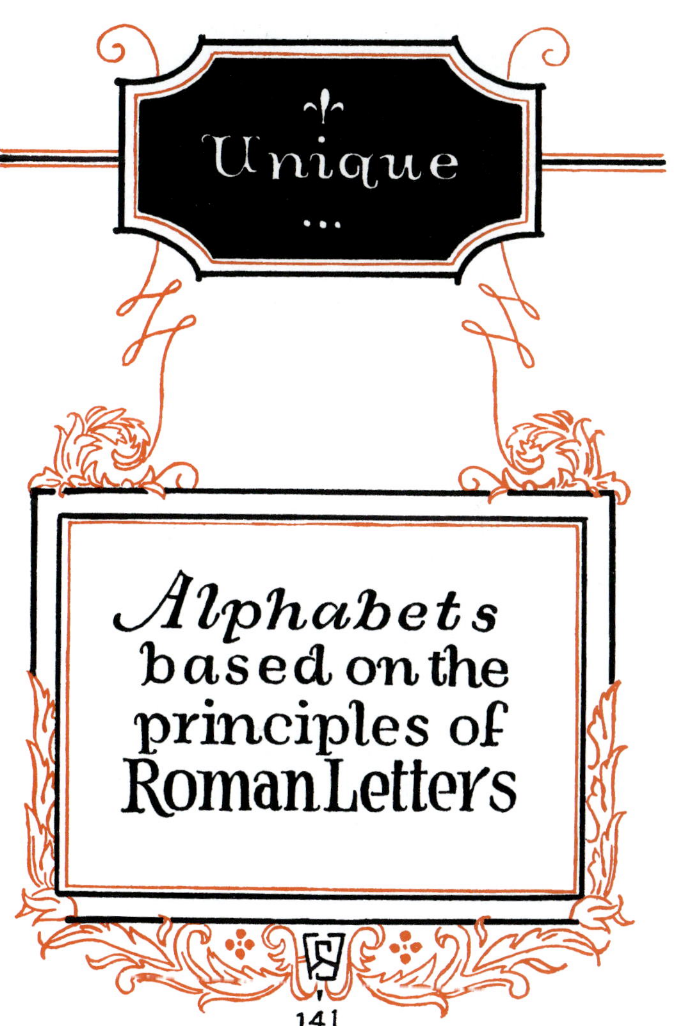
Unique
Alphabets
based on the
principles of
Roman Letters

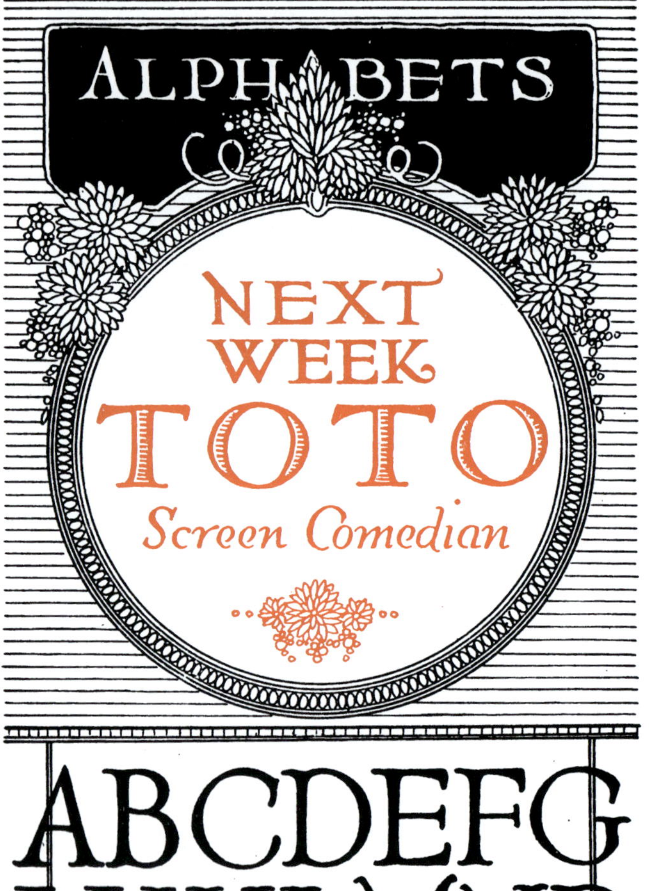

ABCDEFG
HJKLMNP
QRSTUVY

Tuckers Art Title

ABCDE
FGHIJK
LMNOP
QRSTUV
WY~RM
abcdefghijk
lmnopqrsu
tuvvuxyv

ABCDEF
GHIJKLM
NOPQRS
TUVWYZ

abcdefghi
jklmnopr
stuvwyz

ABCDEF
GHIJKLN
MPQRS-
TUVWXY

abcdefghij
klmopqrst
suvvwyyz

ABCDE
FGHIJK
LMNQP
RSTUV
WXYZ&

abcdefghi
jklmnopqr
stuvwxyz

ABCDEF
GHIJKLM
NOPRST
UVY

abcdefghij
klmnopq
rstuvwy

REVISED/

ABCDE
FGHIJK
LMNQRJ
PSTWU

abcdefgh
ijklmnop
qrstuvw

This letter is very good when used small–

ABCDEFG

HIJKLMNO

PQRSTUV

WXYZUV.

abcdeffghiji

klmnopqrst

uvwxyzgrs

WY

ABCDEF
GHIJKLM
NOPQRS
TUVWYZ

abcdefg
hijklmno
pqrstuvw

ABCDEFGHIJ
KLMNOMPQ
RSTUVWYZ
abcdefghijklmn
opqrstuvwy&
123456789

ROUND POSTER

ABCDEFGHIJK
LMNQPRSTU
WX YZ

PHOTOPLAY

ABCDEFGHK

IJLMPNOPQR

SQRSTUTVX

WXYZ

SUB~TITLES

abcdefghijklmn

opqrstuvwyz-

abcdefghknq

rstvwwxy-aah

Goddard
CLASSIC

A B C D E F G
H I J J K L M
N Q P R S T U
V W W X Y Z &
M G S W

abcdeefghhi
jklmmnnop
qrrsſttuuv
wwxxyygz

A Speedball Letter

ABCDEFG
HIJKLMNP
QRSTUVW
XY-MNW&

abcdefghij
klmnopqr
stuvwyzn

ABCDEF
GHJKLM
NOPRST
UVWYZ&:

abcdefghi
jklmnopqr
stuvwxyz
12345678

a few quick alternates

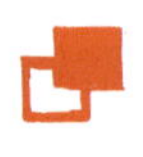

abcdefghijkl
mnopqrstuv
wxyz

abcdefghijkln
opqrstuvwxy
z &

abcdefghijkl
mnopqrstuv
wxyz

aaaaaaaaaaa

abcdefghijkl
mnnmnopqrsttu
uvwwxyz&
abcdefghghij
klmnopqrstuvu
wwxyz

Squat Lower Case

abcdefghij
klmnopqr-
stuvuyxz ~

F.Y.

ABCDEFGHIJK
LMNOPQRSTUV
WXYZ

GOTHIC

ABCDEFGHIJK
LMNOPQRSTU
VWXYZ

ROMAN

ABCDEFGHIJK
LMNOPQRSTU
VWXYZ

ITALIC

ABCDEFGHJ
KLMNOPQRST
UVWXY

DE VINNE

ABCDEFGH
IJKLMNOPQ
RSTUVWYZ

abcdefghijkln
opqrstuvwxy

abcdefghijkln
opqrstuvwxy

a continuous and
runninghand curve

HAMILTON

ABCDEFGHI
JKLMNOPQR
STUVWXYZ
GKMNRSWB

abcdefghijk
lmnopqrst
uvwxymrg

ABCDEFG
HIJKLMN
OPQRST
UVWXYZ

abcdefgr
hijklmpq
stuvwxy

from

GOTHIC

Commonly called "Spurred Gothic"

ABCDEFI
GHJKLMN
OQPRSTUV
WXYZ - - - -

abcdefgh
ijkmnopq
stuvwxy

ABCDE
FGHIJKL
MNOPQ
RSTUVW
XYZ

abcdefghi
jklmnoprt
qsuvwyx

At'a BOY~

ABCDE

FGHJK

LMNOP

RSTUV

~WY~

abcdefghi

jklmnopr

stuvy~

ABCDE
FGHIJK
LMNOP
RSTUVY

abcdef-
ghijklm
opqrstu
vwxyz

ABCDEF
GHIJKM
NOPRST
UVWXY

PLAIN GOTHIC

ABCDEFGHIJ
KLMNOPRST
UVXYZW&

HEAVY AND THIN- - - - -

ABCDEFG
HIJKLMN
OPQRSTU
VWXYZ&'
12345678
abcdefghij
klmpqrstts

POWER

ABCDEF
GHIJKLN
MQPRS
TUVWY

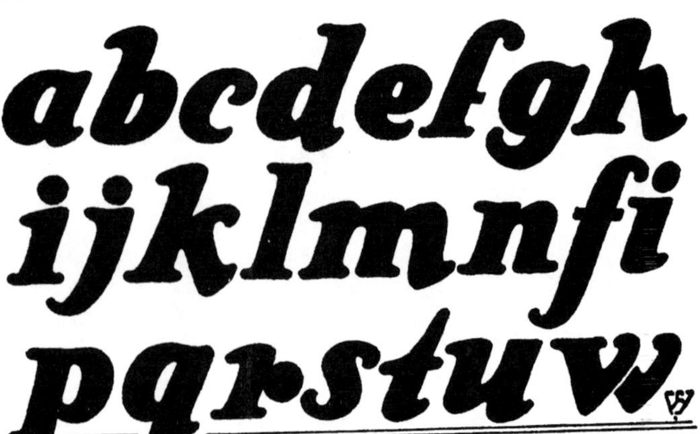

Bold Italic

ABCDE
FFGHIJ
KLMNQ
PRSTU
TUVWY

lowercase

aabcde
fghijkl
mnopq
rstuvr
wxywz

Caps for the two *lower-cases* that follow-by altering the serif

ABCD
EFGH
JKLM
NPRS
TUW

abcde

fghijk

lmno,

prstu

vwyz

abcde

fghijk

lmnop

qrstuv

wxyz

Upper-case followed by Lower-case~

ABCDE

FGHIJK

LMNOP

QRSTU

VWXY

WS

abcdef
ghijkl
mnopq
rstuv!,
wxyz

abcdefg
hijkmno
pqrstuv
wxy
erfwkst

Strong

ABCDEF
GHIJKL
MNOPQR
STUWY
abcdefgh
ijklmnop
qrstuvw

Money is-
one thing
that talks

ABCDEF
GHIJKL
MNQPR
STUVY-
it's-cheap-

But the Question is – Are you making any money?

abcdefgh ijklmno- pqrstuv- don't ask!

Squat

ABCD
EFGH
IJKLM
NOPQR
STUV
WXY~

abcdefgh
ijklmnop-
qrstuvyz.

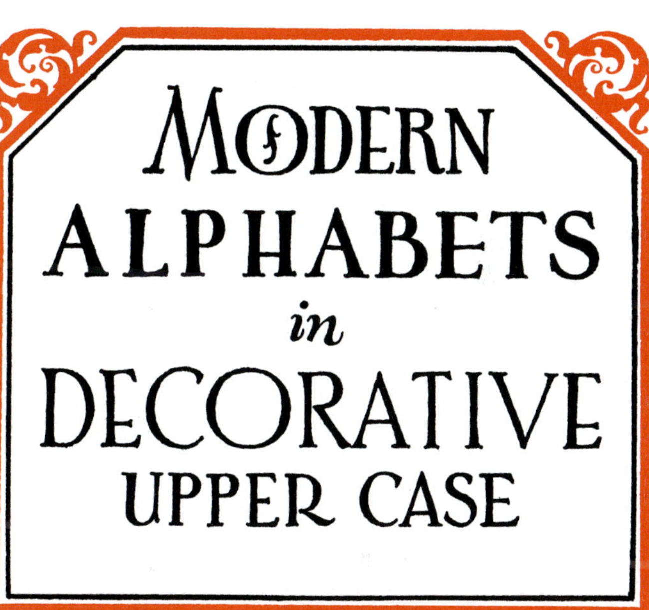
MODERN
ALPHABETS
in
DECORATIVE
UPPER CASE

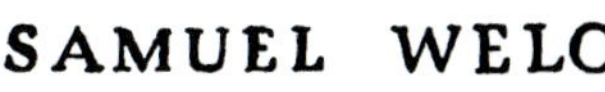
SAMUEL WELO

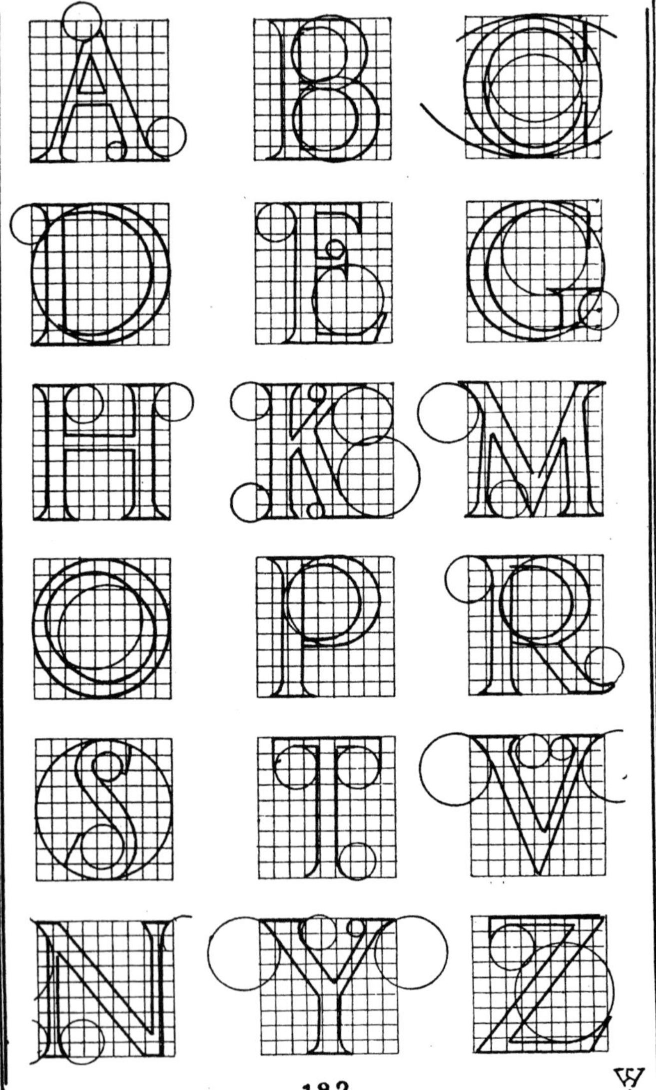

ABCDE
FGHJKL
MNOPR
STUWXY

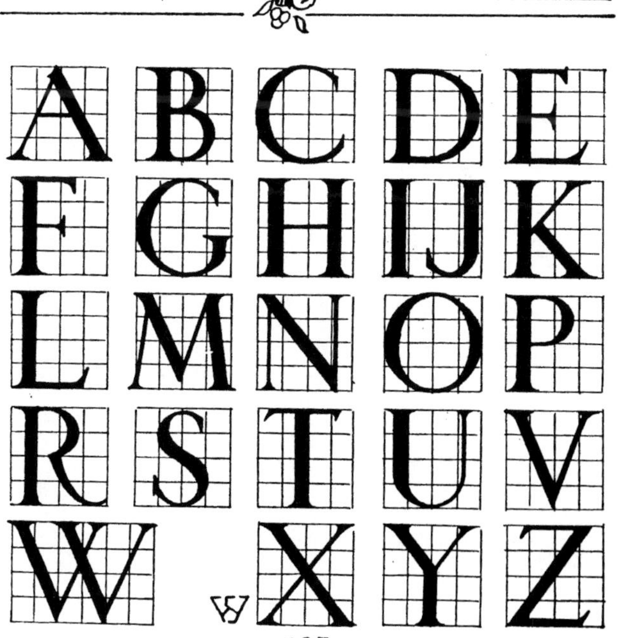

Italian Renaissance

ABCDE
FGHIJKL
MNPQR
·STUV·

"ROMAN CLASSIC"

ABCDEFG
HJKLMNO
RSTWXYZ

A B C D E F
G H I J K L M
N O P R S U Y
Q T V X W Z

A B C D E
F G H I J L
K L M O P
N Q R S T
U V W Y X

ABCDEF
GHJKLM
PQRSTV
WXYZ&

ÆBCDEF
GHIJJKM
LNOPQR
STUVWX
YZ Plakat

DO YOU LIKE THIS STYLE

· · ·

· MOTHER ·
· WIPES · THE ·
TEARS · AWAY
she knows
· HOW~TOO ·

· · ·

ABCDEFGHIJ
KLMNOPQRS
· TUVWXYZ ·

ABCDE

FGHIJK

LMNM

NOPQR

STUV

WWXY

ABCDE

FGHIJK

LMNOP

QRSTU

VWMN

XYZY

ABCDE
FGHIJKL
MNOQP
RSTUV
WX & YZ
MNRY

Oswald Cooper

ABCDE

GHIJKL

MNOP

QRST

UVWY

RMSW

ABCDE
FGHIJK
LMNOP
RSTUV
WXYZ&

Style of finish shown here adds to variety

FY

Type

FROM FORUM

ABCDE

FGHIJK

LMNOP

RSTUV

WXYZ&

MODIFIED

ABCDE

FGHIJK

LMNQP

RSTUV

WMWX

YRNKZ

ABCD
EEFGI
HJJKL
MQRS
TUXY
WZ3.&
Questions,

WY

WHY YOU SHOULD PATRONIZE

ABCD
EFGH
IJKLM
NORS
TUWY

ABCD
EFGHI
JKLM
NOPR
STUW

ABCD
EFGHIJ
KLMN
PQRW
STUY

ROMAN CAPS

With a strong Classical feeling

ECK

ABCDE
FGHIJK
LMNOP
QRSTU
VWXYZ

THESE MAY HELP

ANKMN
RSUWY

ABCD
EFGHI
JKLM
NOPQ
RSTU
WYZ

POSTER

ABCD
EFGHIJ
KLMN
OPQR
STUV
WXYZ

A BOLD POSTER

ABCD
EFGHIJ
KLMN
OPQR
STUV
WXYZ

A HEAVY ONE

ABCD
EFGH
IJKL
MNOP
QRST
UVWY

The Odd One

The Coast of Folly

abcdefg
hijklmpr
stuwxy
to q ro

ABCDE
FGHIJKL
MNPQR
STUWY

abcdefg
hijklmnp
rstuvwz

ABCDEF

GHJKLM

NOPRST

UVWYZ

ABCDEFG

HJKLMNO

PRSTUVW

abcdefghikmoprst

ABCDEF
GHIJKLM
NOPRST
UVXY

ABCDEFG
HIJKLMNO
PRSTUVW
XYZ

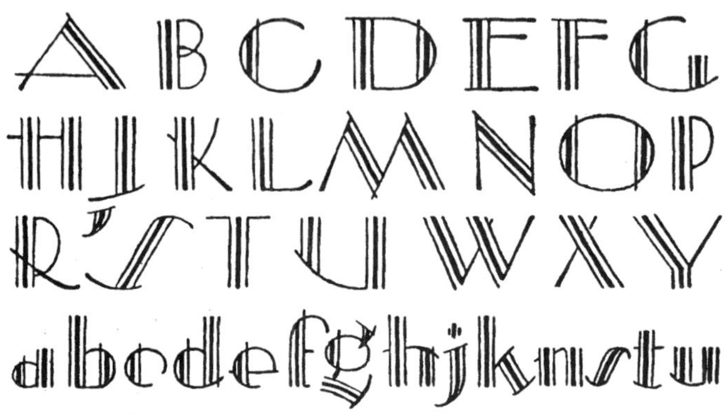

ABCDEFG
HJKLMNOP
RSTUWXY

ABCDEFGHIJ
KLMNQPRS
TUWXYZ
abcdefghiklmprstu

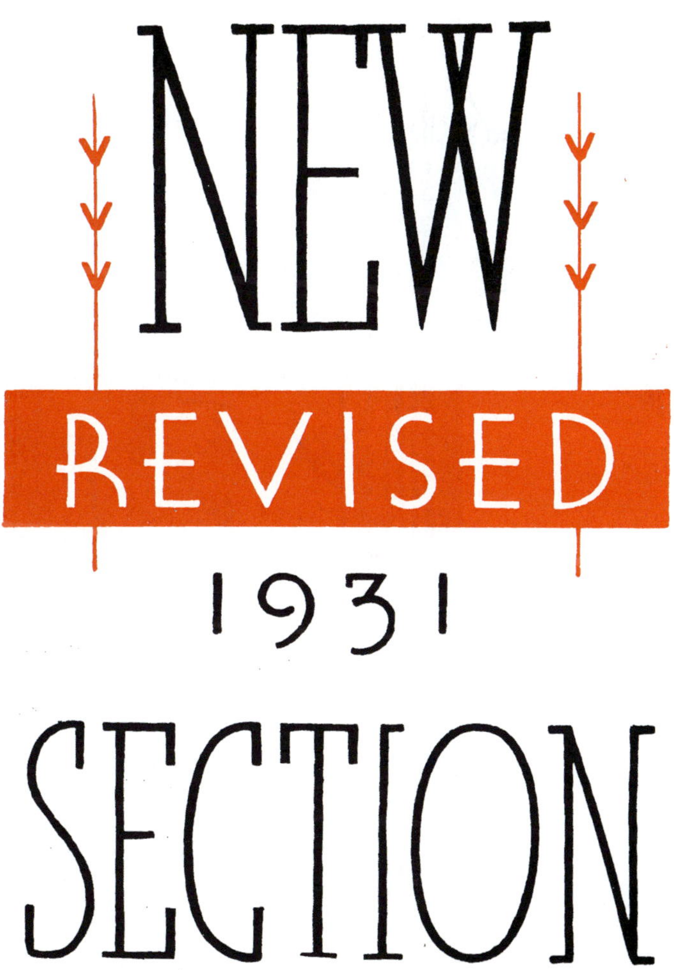
NEW
REVISED
1931
SECTION

GET ▲ ▲

GIVE ▲

▲ ▲ ▲ ▲ *The*

FOLLOWING
PAGES GIVE
new THOUGHT
IN MODERN
DESIGN ▲

MODERNISTIC

FOR *use* IN COLOR

SPOTS

208 C

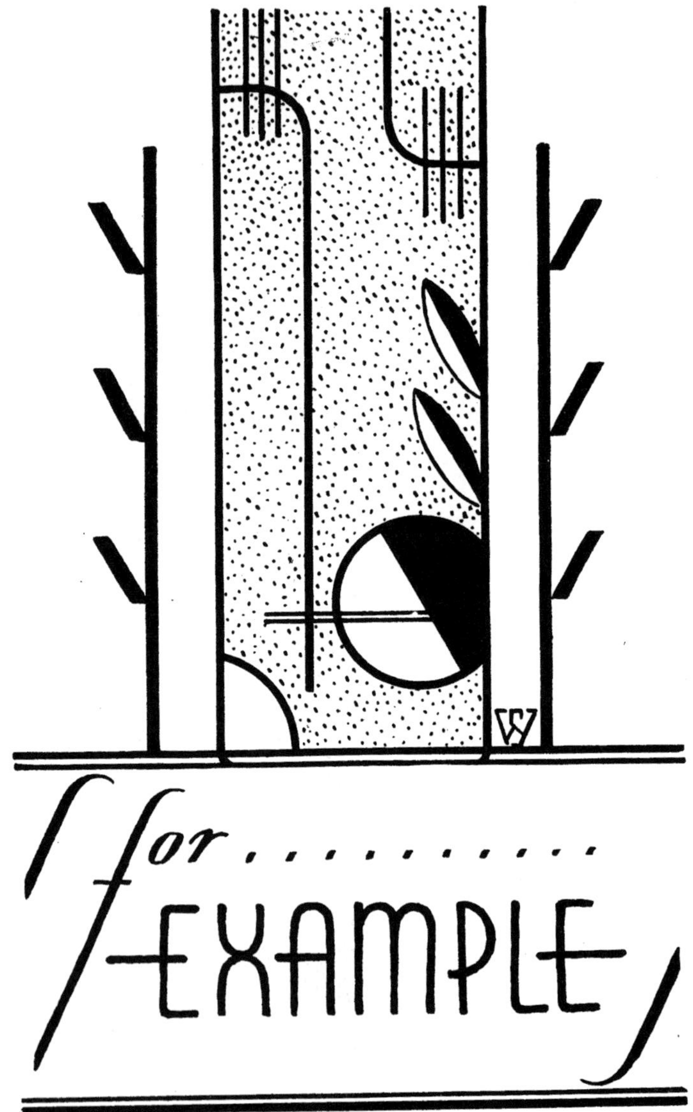

208 D

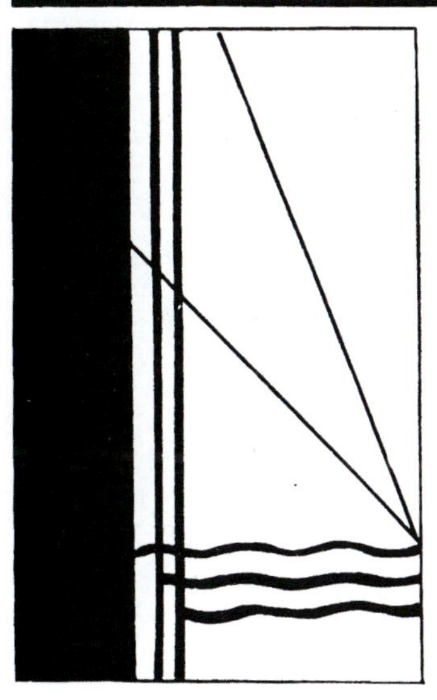

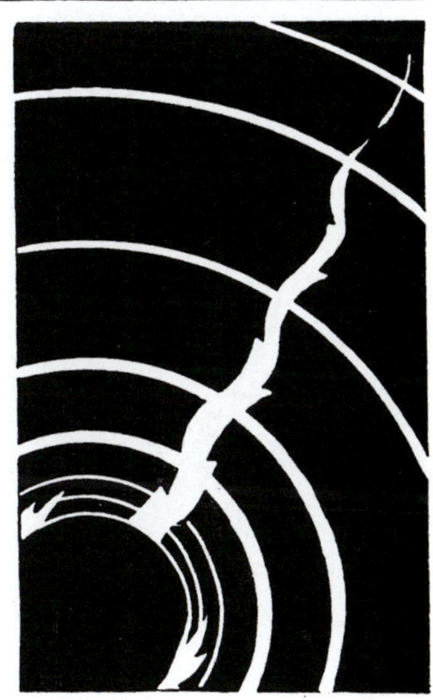

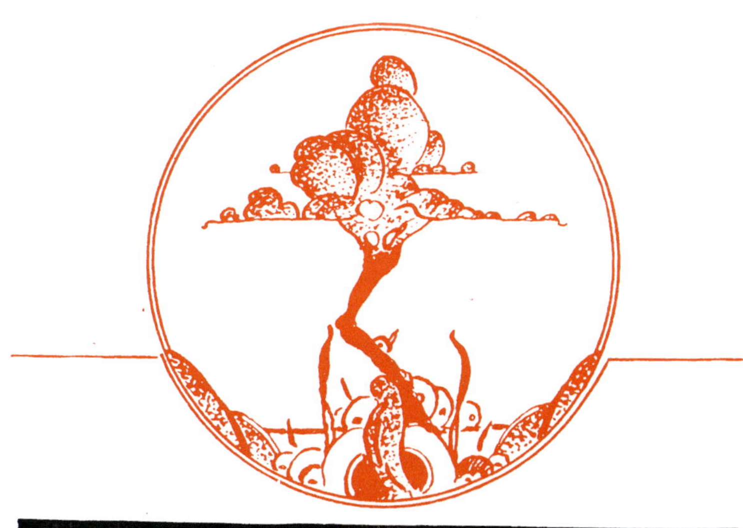

208. E

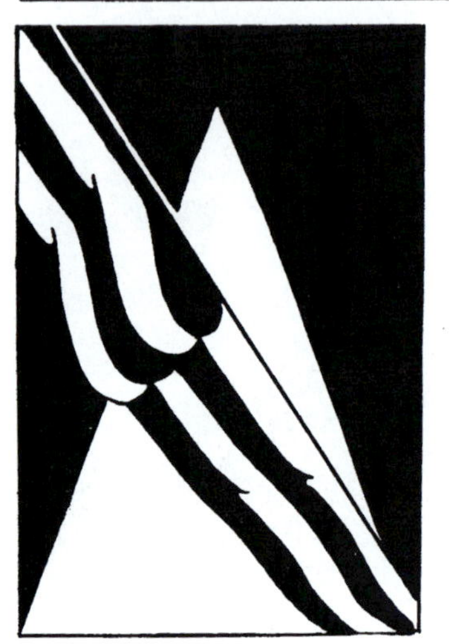

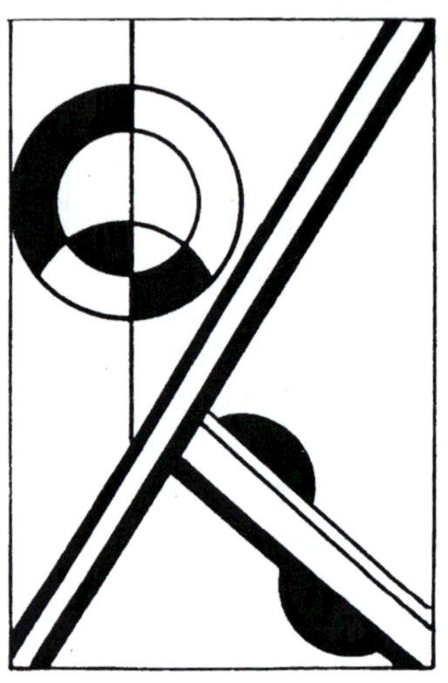

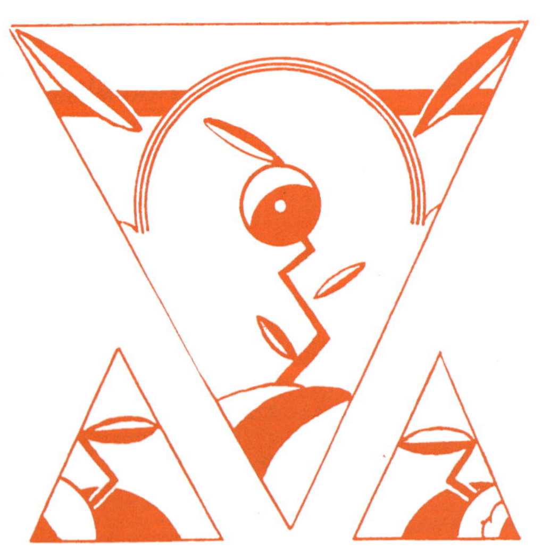

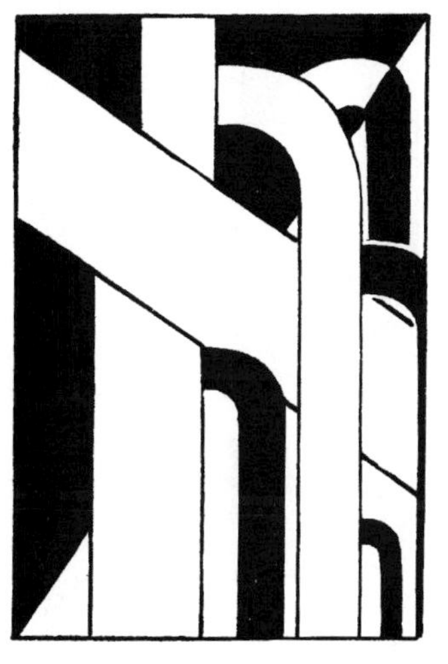

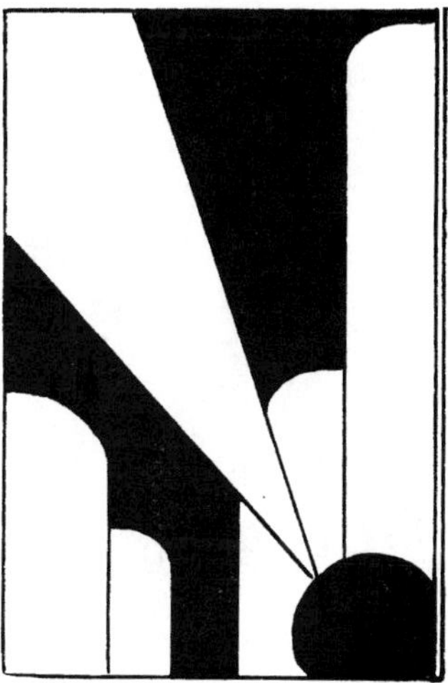

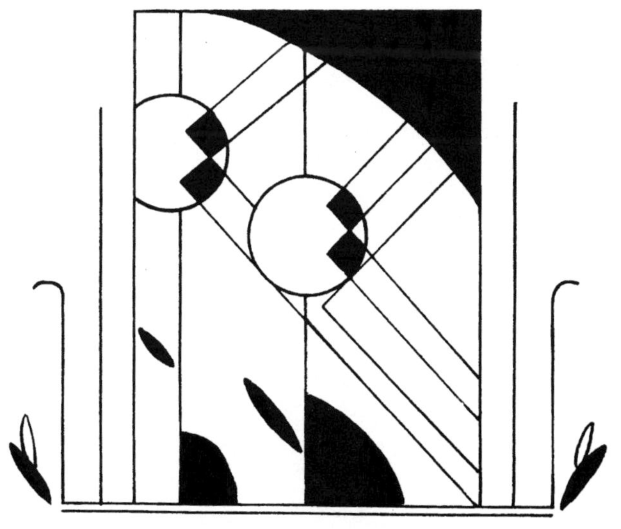

208 G

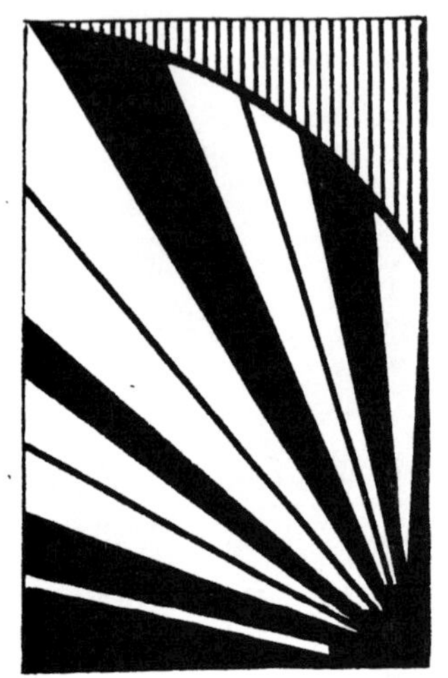

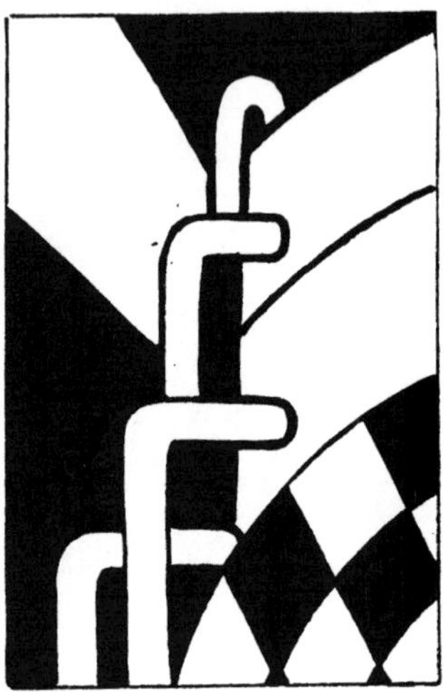

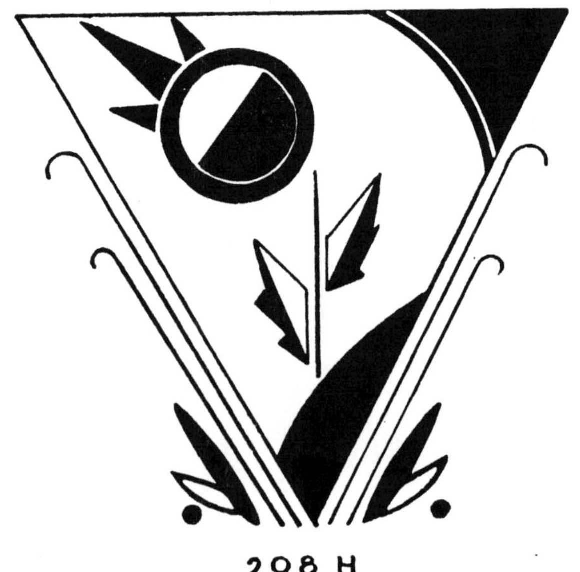

208 H

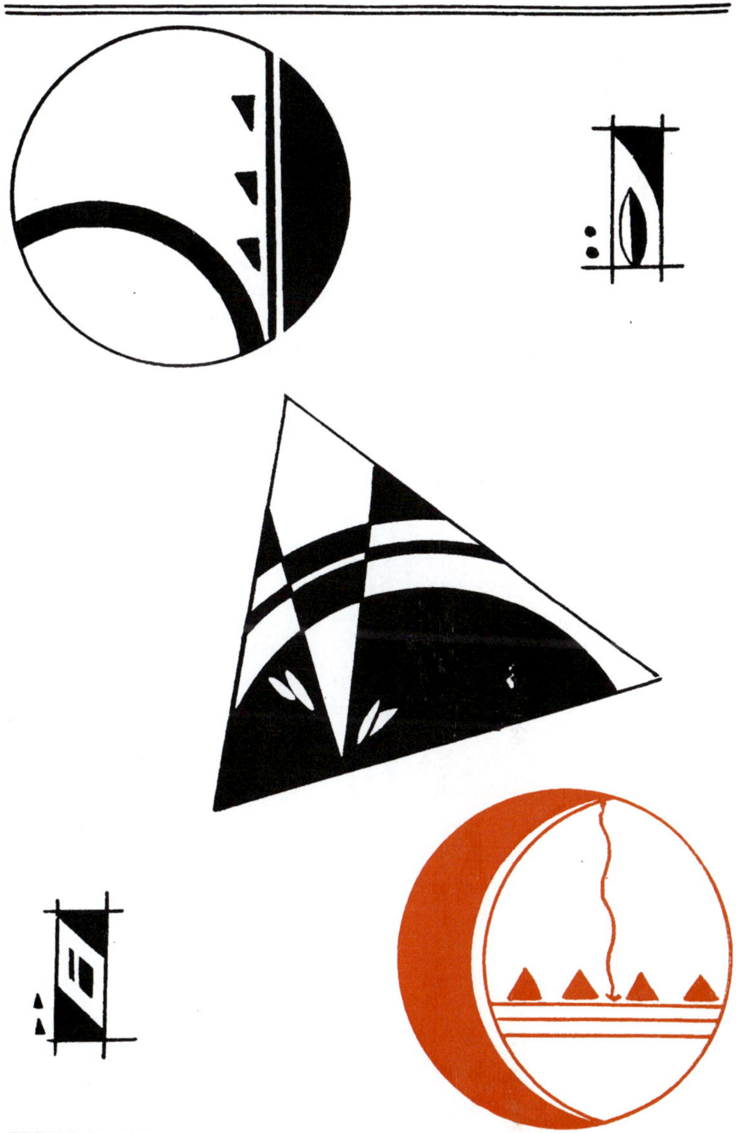

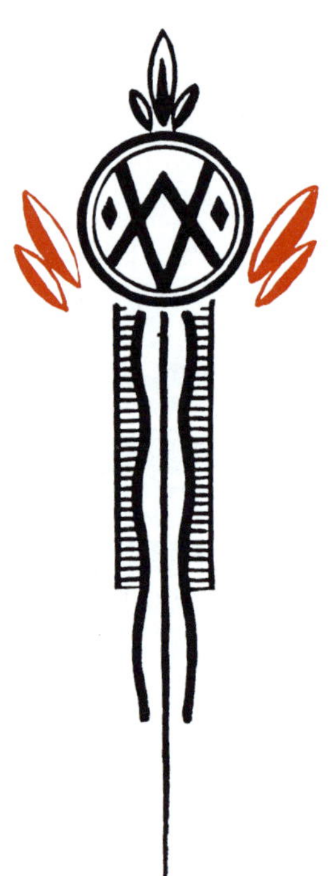

208 J

for color

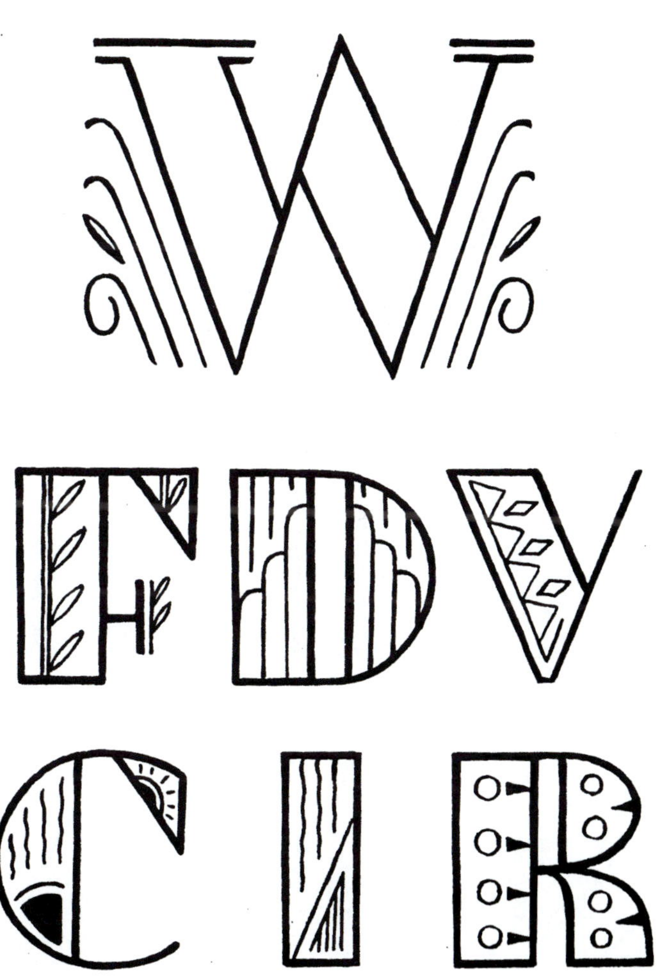

208 K

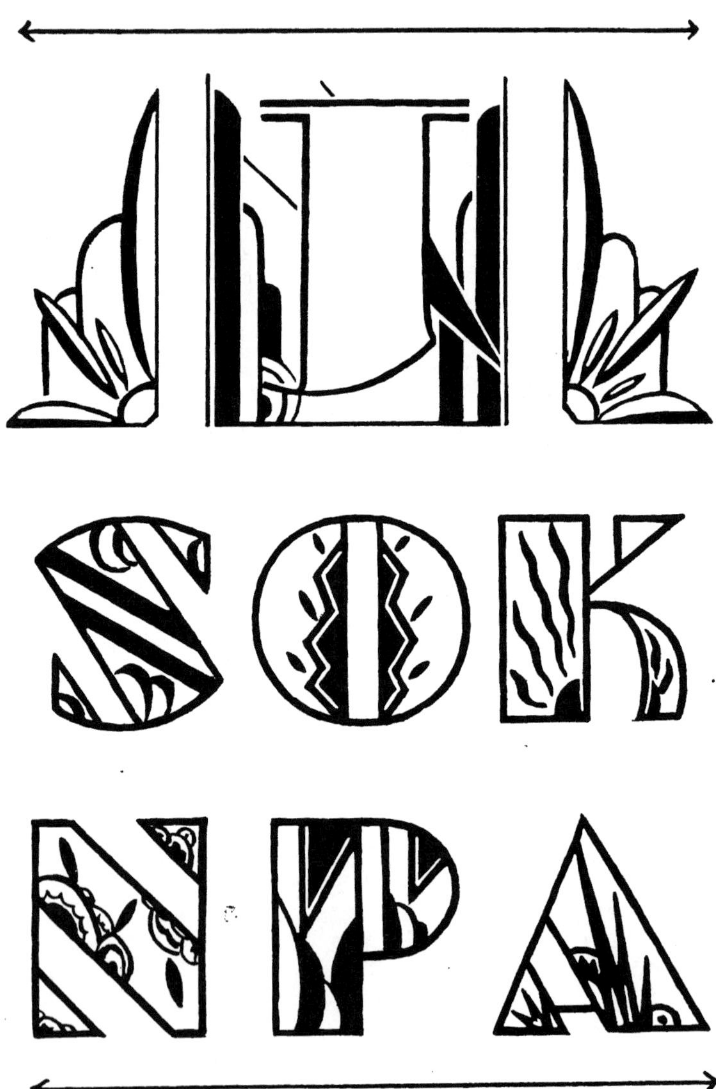
208L

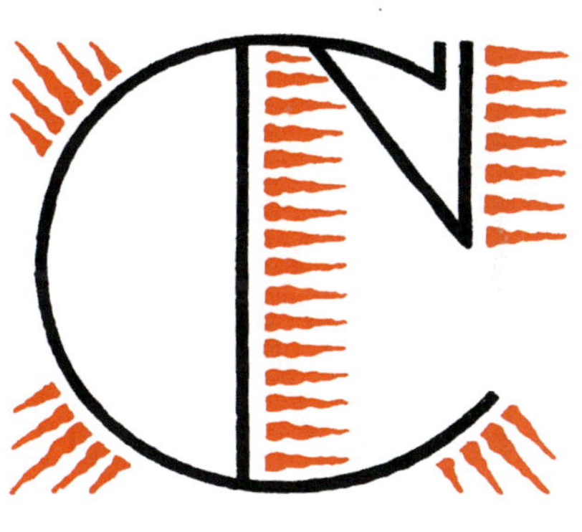

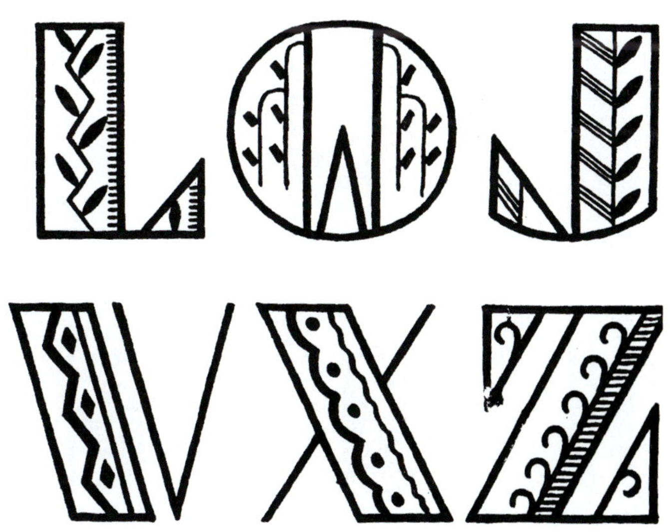

208 M

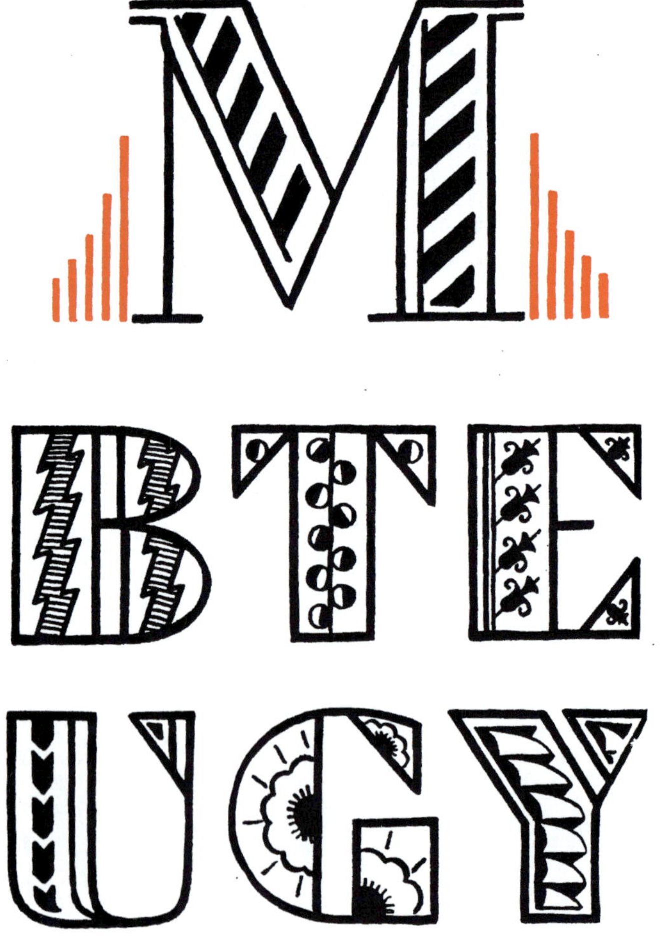

208 N

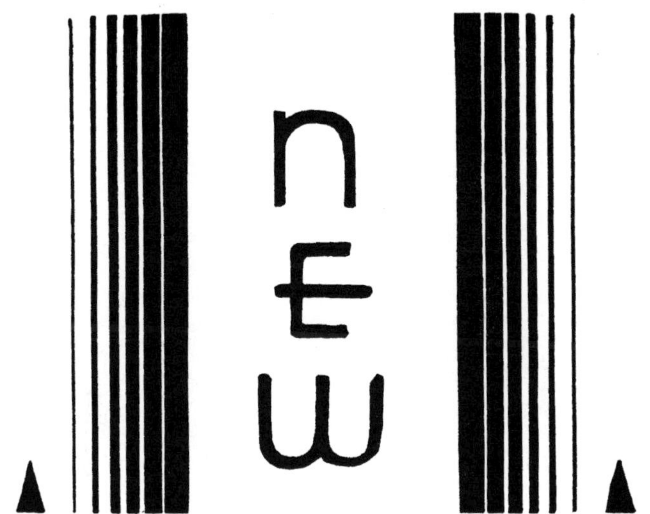

ALPHABETS ARE HERE

208 O

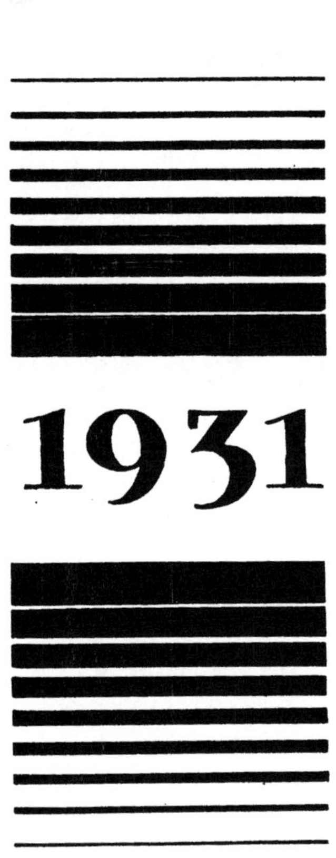

208 P

THESE NEW

ABCDE

FGHIJK

LMNOP

QRSTU

VWXY

PRICES

208 Q

THESE ARE

ABCDE
FGHIJK
LMNOP
QRSTU
VWXY
FOR SALE

208 R

ABCD

EFGH

JKLM

NOP

RSTU

VWXY

208 S

ABCD
EFGH
IJKLM
NOPQ
RSTU
V W X

208 T

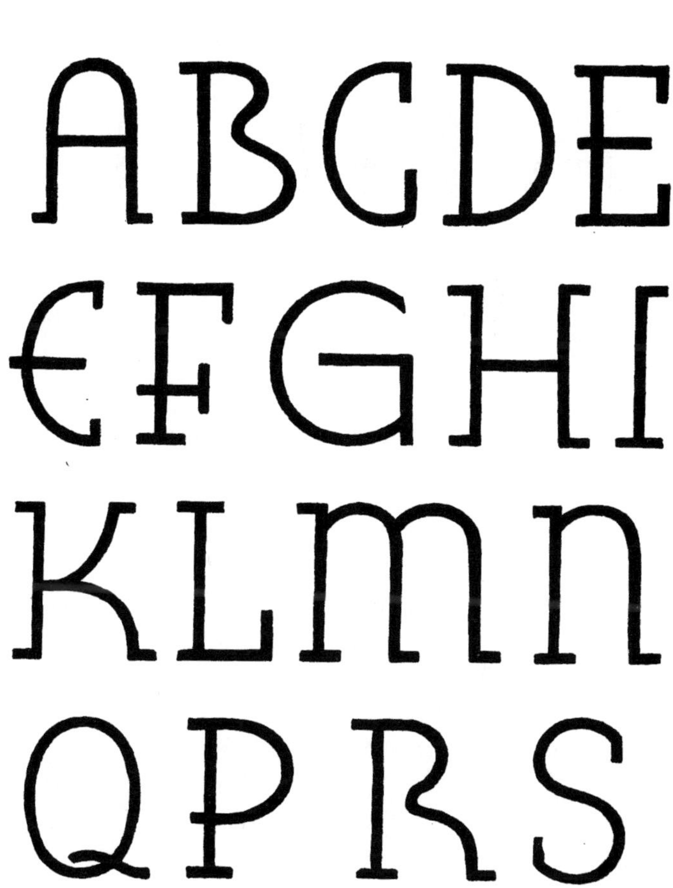

ABCDE

EFGHI

KLMN

QPRS

VWXY

208 U

A B C D

E F G H

J K L M

N O P Q

R S T U

V W X Y

208 V

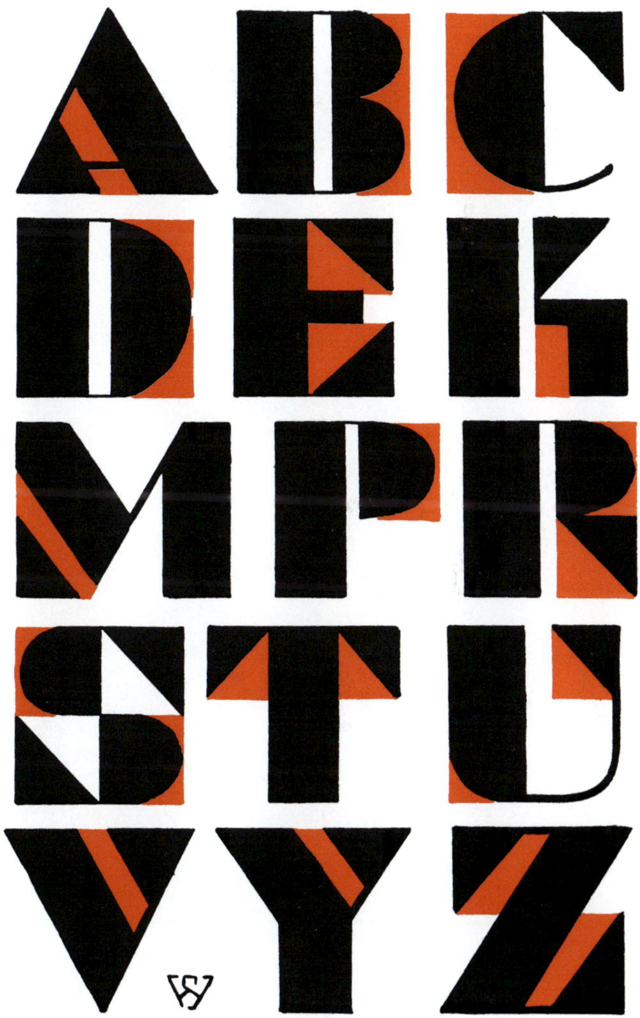

208 W

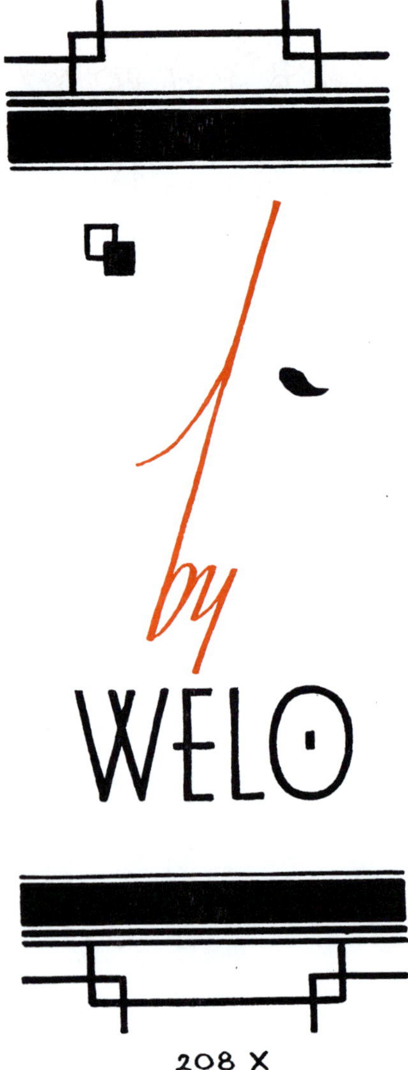

208 X

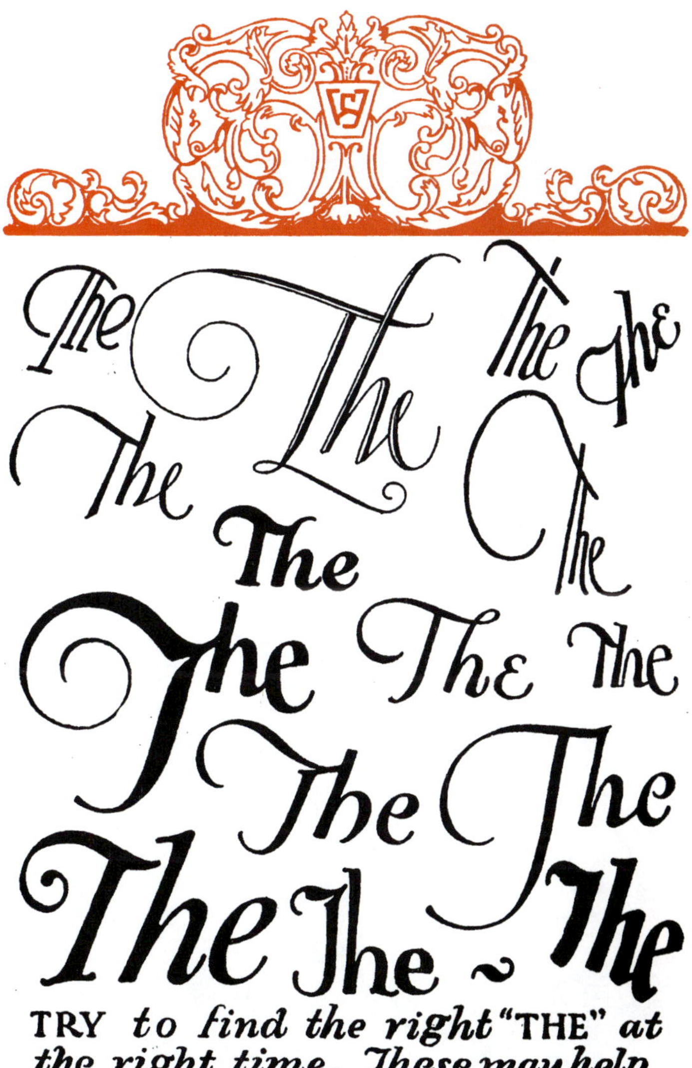

TRY *to find the right* "THE" *at the right time, These may help*

The The The

The The The The

The The The The

The The The

The The The The

The The The

The The The The

The The The

The The
The
The The The
The The The
The The
The
The The
The
The The The
The
The The The

The The The

The The The

The The The The

The The The

The The! The

The The The The

The The

The The The The

The The The

TradeMarks

Some of the best~ *TradeMarks* are those which use combinations of letters or abstract symbols with no attempt to strive for illustrative material. It is gratifying to note the remarkable amount of clever study that goes into the designing of the *trade-marks* today~~ *The* fact is important that few designers ~ have let their striving for beauty run away with the "*utility*" thought

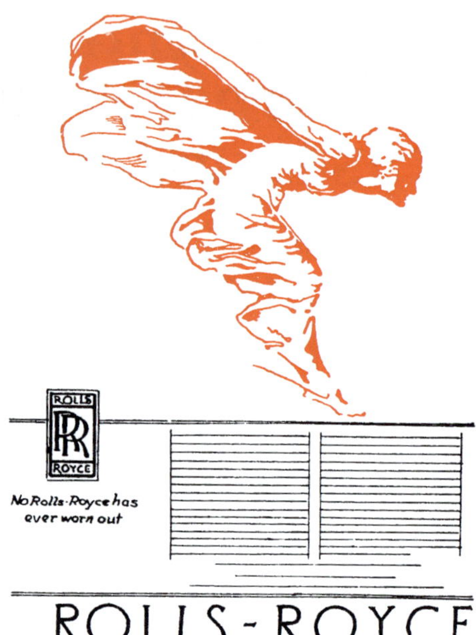

A FIGURETTE THAT TELLS THE "ROLLS-ROYCE" STORY AND CONSEQUENTLY HAS VIRTUALLY BECOME A TRADE MARK

The Rolls-Royce, when it first started business, settled upon a trade mark in the form of the two R's, intertwined.

Not long ago a beautiful silver figurette was placed on the radiator cap of the car; the poised figure of a woman, balanced on one foot, body flung far forward and flying draperies indicative of easy, swift flight.

A single advertisment appeared in which this figure was featured in the pictorial display. It appealed at once. "a new trade mark now before the public." WJ

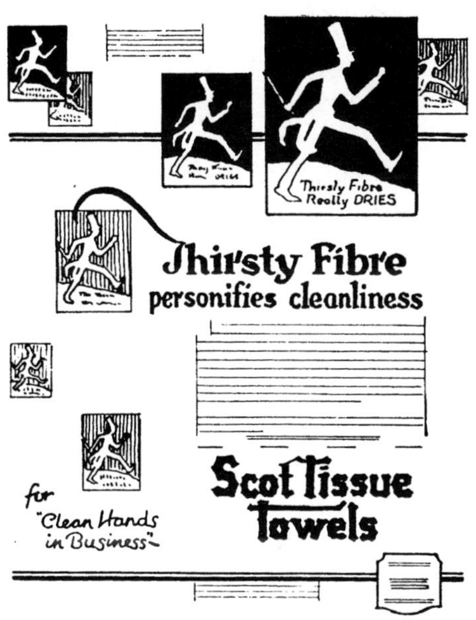

AN EXAMPLE OF THE REPETITION IDEA USED FOR STRESSING TRADE CHARACTER ONLY

Trade-Marks

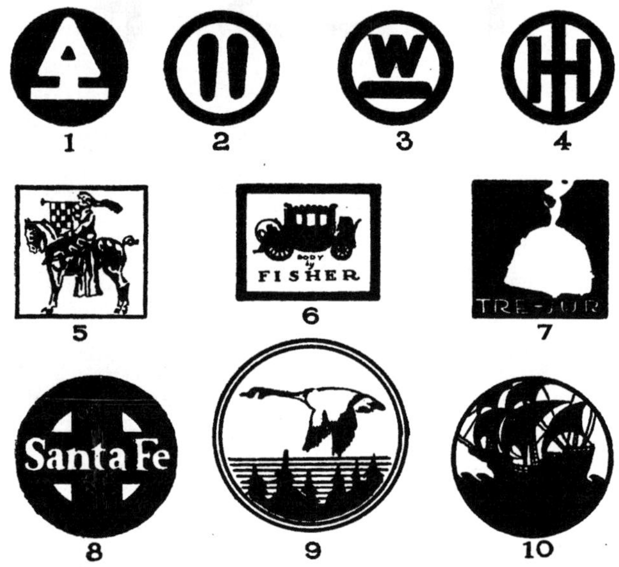

(1) LEE TIRE & RUBBER CO. N.Y. (4) THE OHIO STEEL FOUNDRY CO. LIMA, O

A few of the most striking American *trade-marks*, illustrate nicely how far this country has advanced in *trade-mark* design.

MONOGRAMS

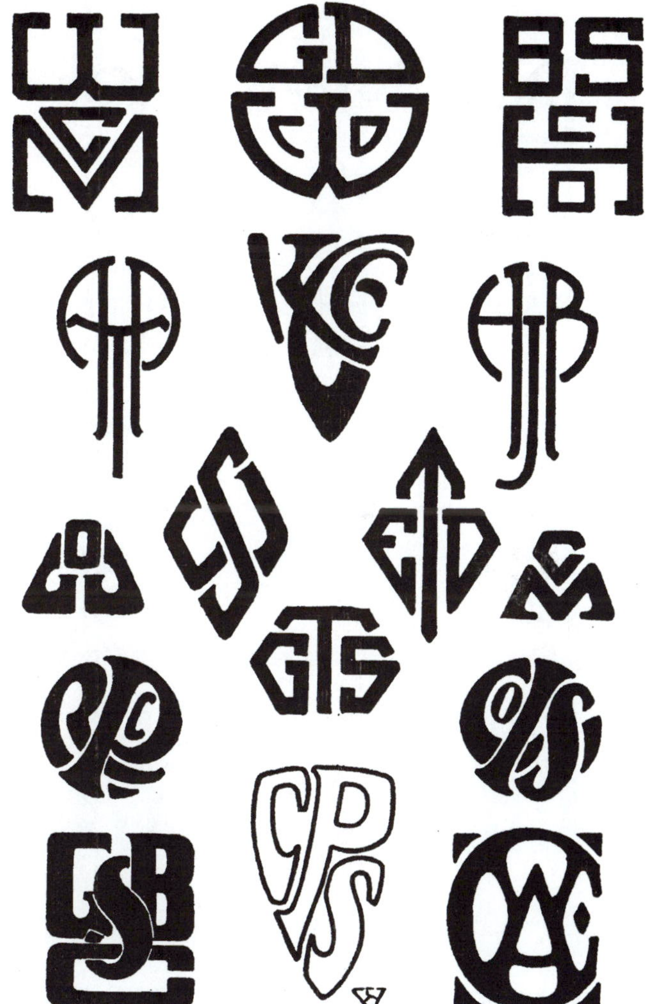

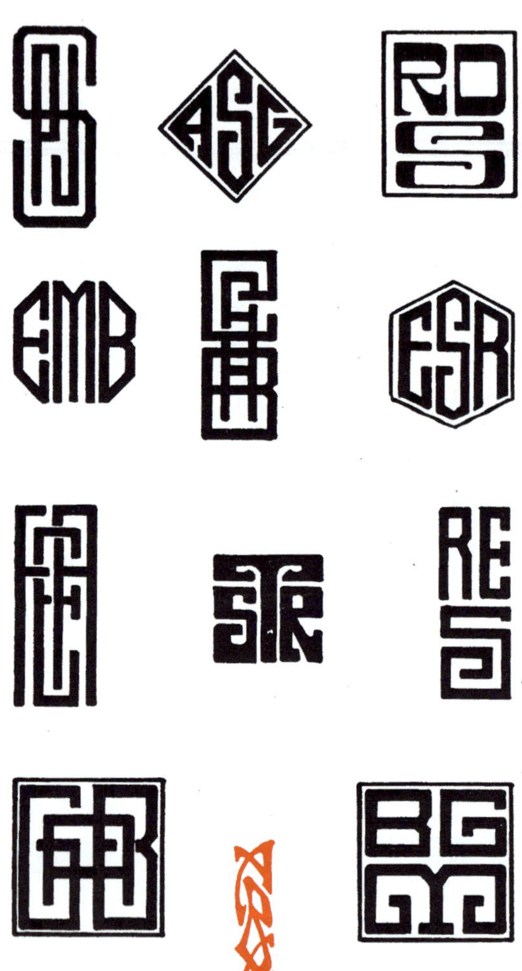
ASG
EMB
ESR

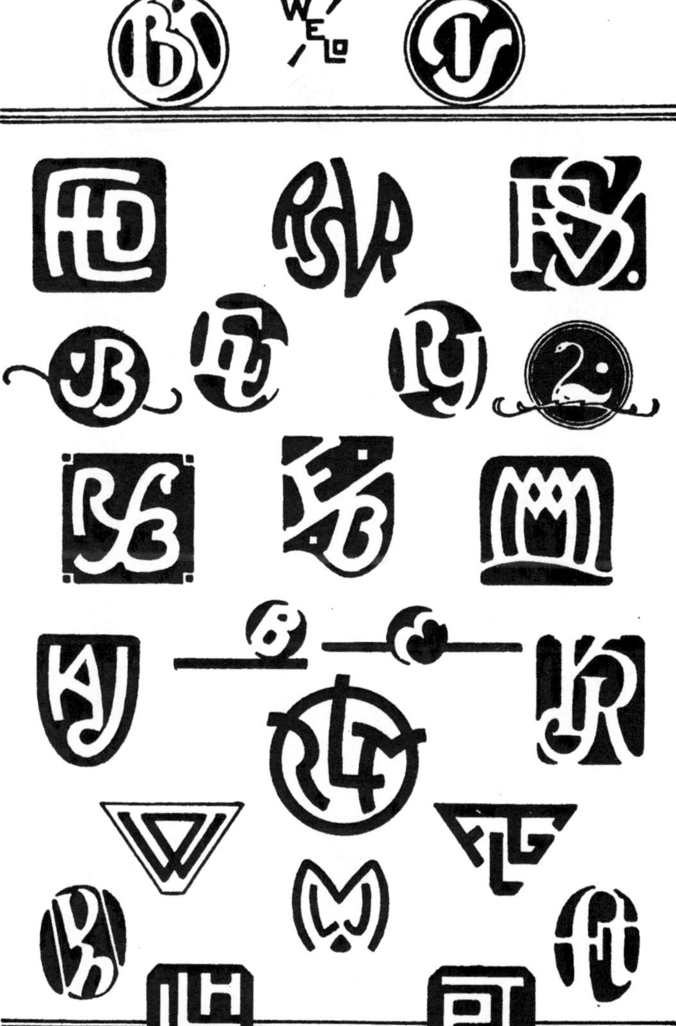

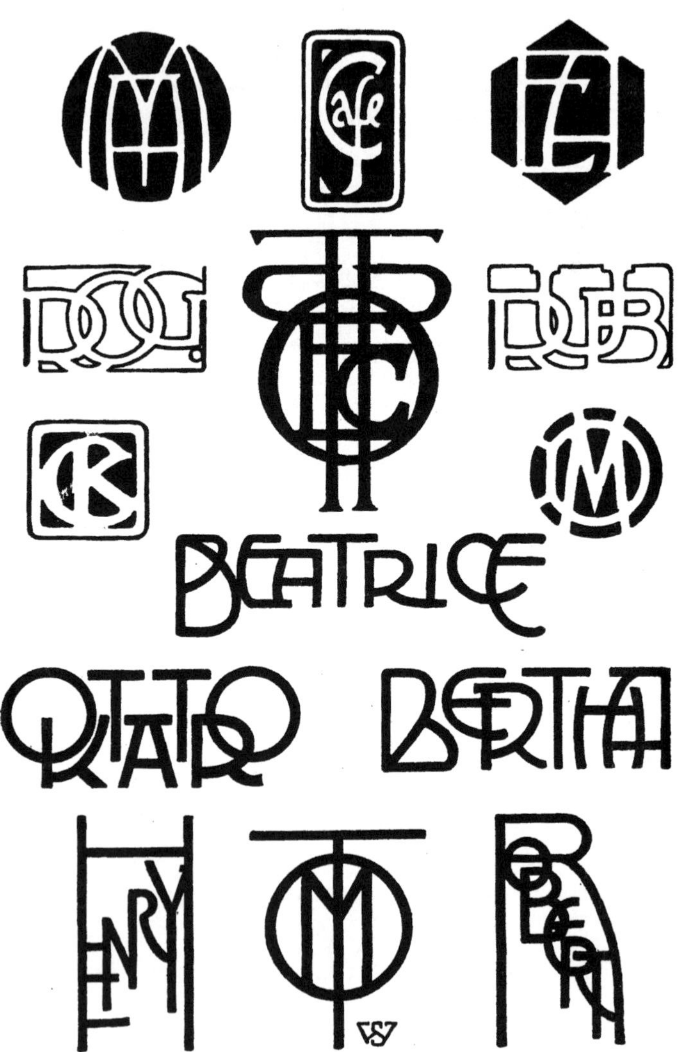
Cafe
BEATRICE
BERTHA
HENRY
ROBERT

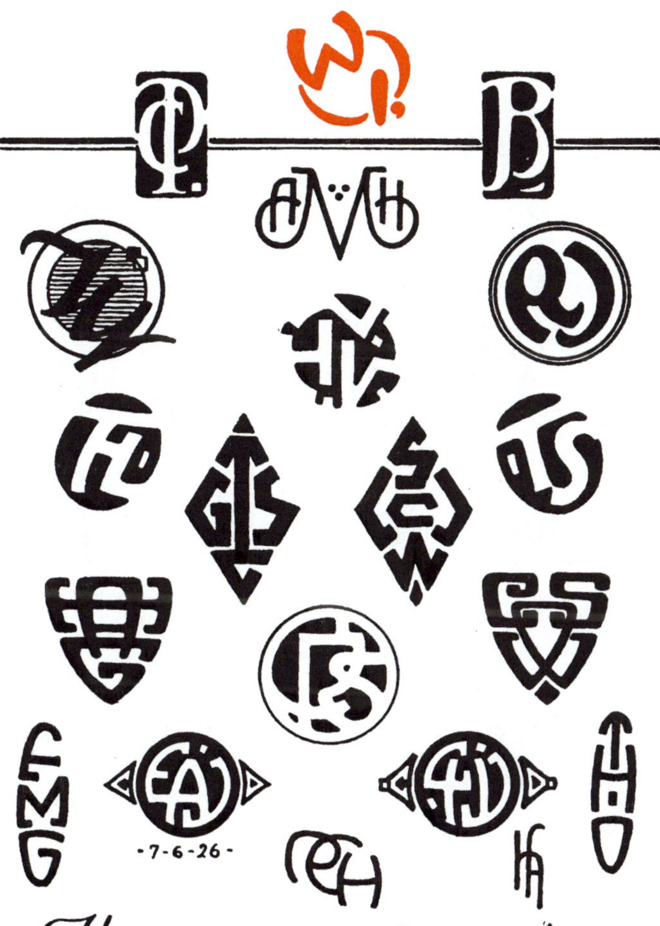

The time is often when the smallest kind of a hunch would do the trick ~ ~

Question Mark

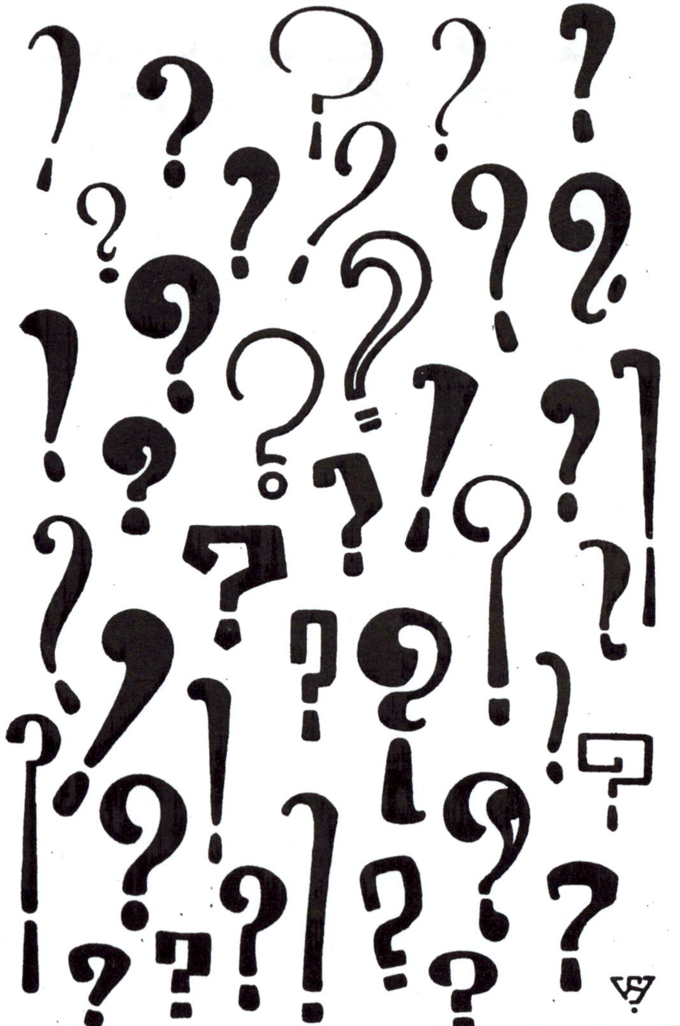

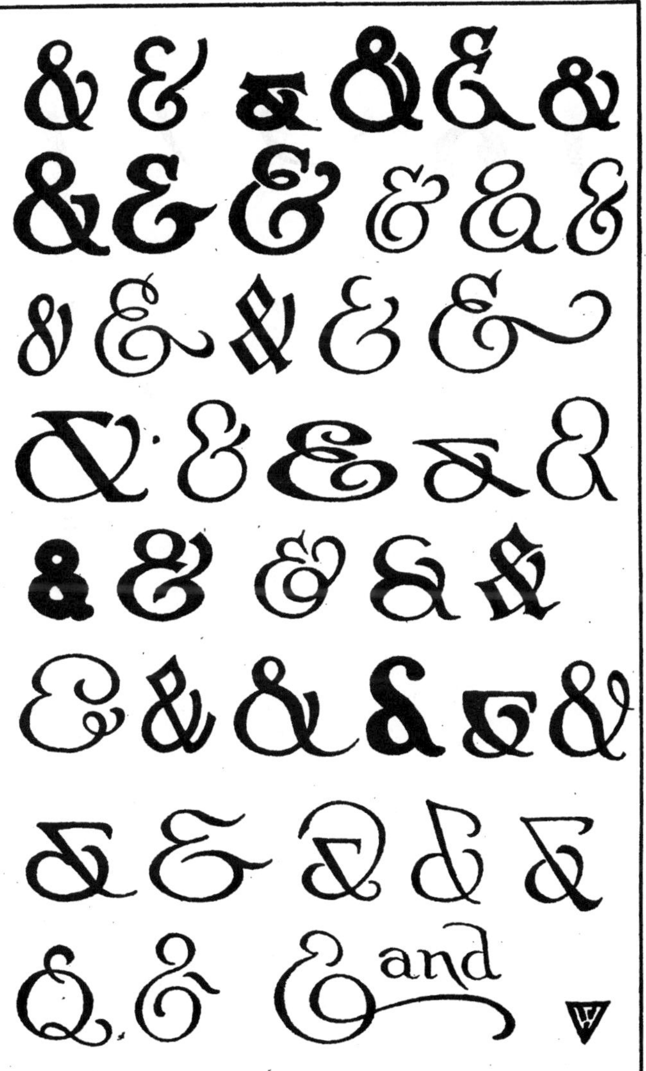
and

ROMAN

- MCMXXV -

I II III IV V VI VII

VIII IX X XI XII XIII

XIV XV XVI XVII

XVIII XIX XX - - -

XXX XL L LX LXX
30 40 50 60 70

LXXX XC C - CC
80 90 100 200

CCC - CD - D - DC
300 400 500 600

DCC DCCC CM - M
700 800 900 1000

NUMERALS

NUMERALS

12345678

123456789

12345678

12345678

12345678

123456789

12345678

12345678

123456789

123456789-

123456789

123456789

123456789

12345678

12345678-

123456789

123456789

123456789$

123456789

123456789

123456789

123456789

123456789

123456789

12345678!
123456789
123456789
123456789
123456789
123456789&
123456789
12345678!
123456789

123456789

123456789

123456789

123456789

1234567-9

123456789

123456789

123456789

123456789

123456789

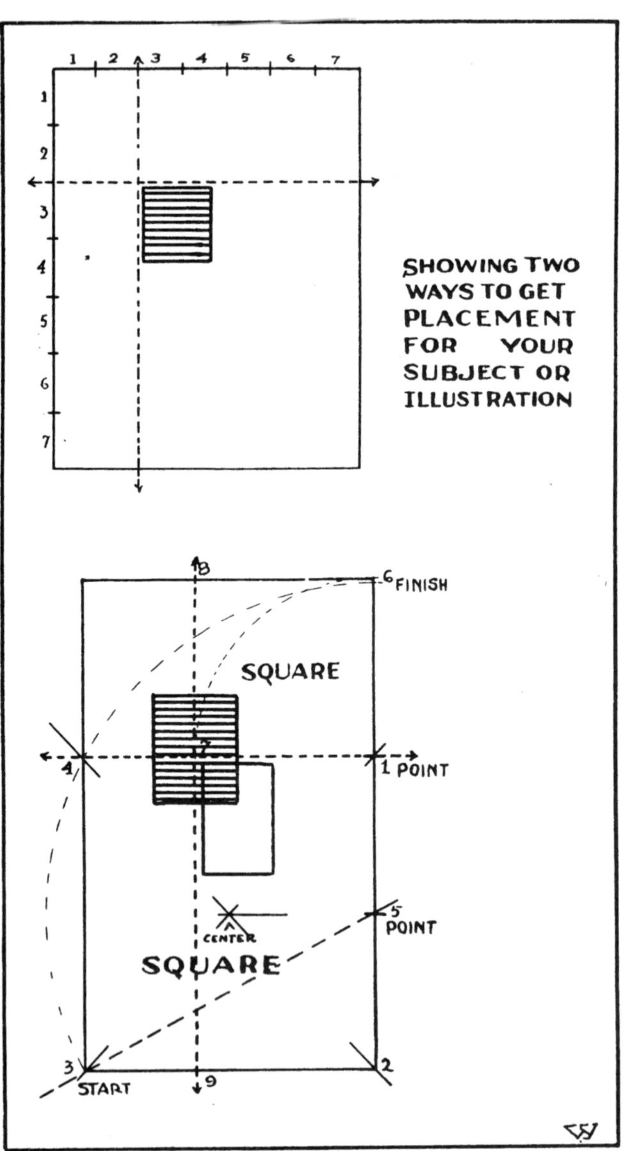
1
2
3
4
5
6
7
1
2
3
4
5
6
7
SHOWING TWO WAYS TO GET PLACEMENT FOR YOUR SUBJECT OR ILLUSTRATION
8
6 FINISH
SQUARE
4
1 POINT
5 POINT
CENTER
SQUARE
3
START
9
2

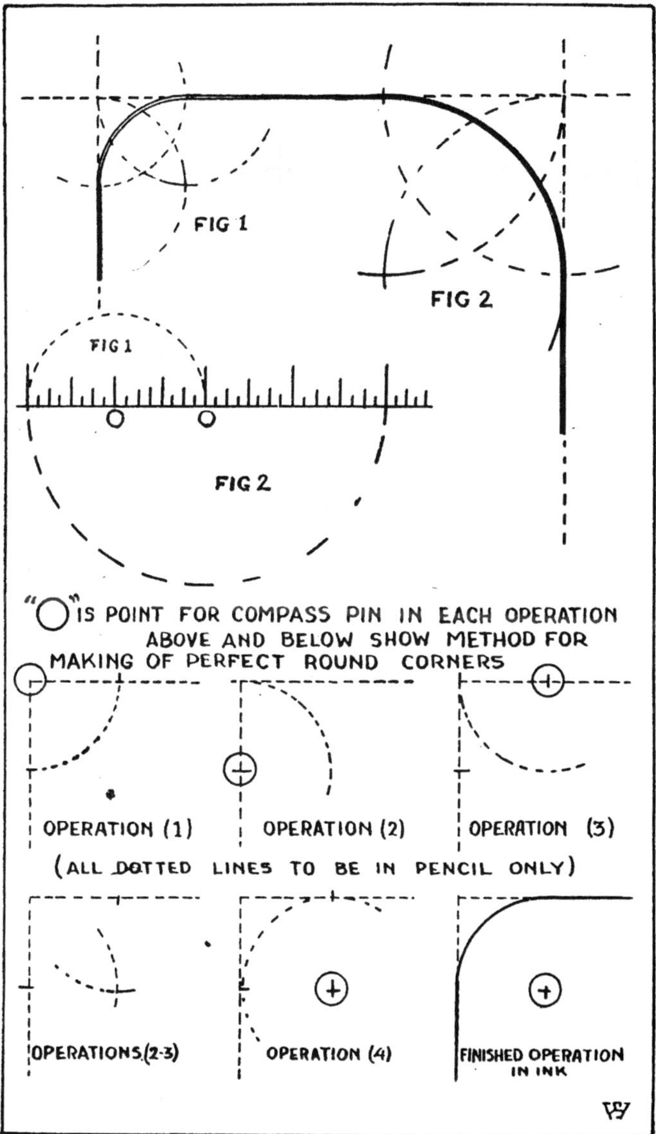
FIG 1
FIG 2
FIG 1
FIG 2
"O" IS POINT FOR COMPASS PIN IN EACH OPERATION
ABOVE AND BELOW SHOW METHOD FOR
MAKING OF PERFECT ROUND CORNERS
OPERATION (1)
OPERATION (2)
OPERATION (3)
(ALL DOTTED LINES TO BE IN PENCIL ONLY)
OPERATIONS (2-3)
OPERATION (4)
FINISHED OPERATION
IN INK

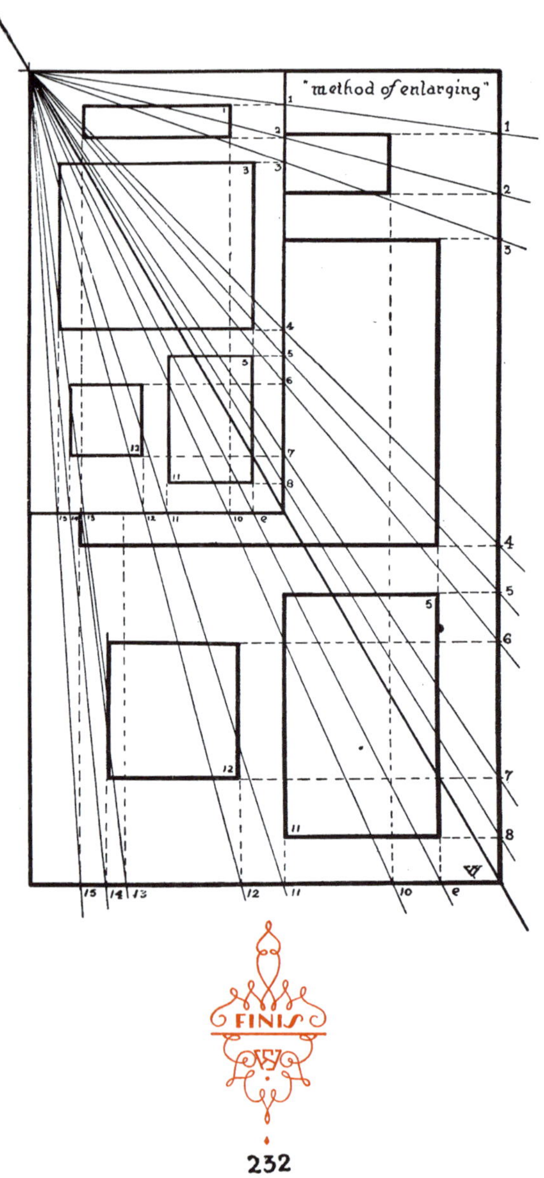
"method of enlarging"
FINIS

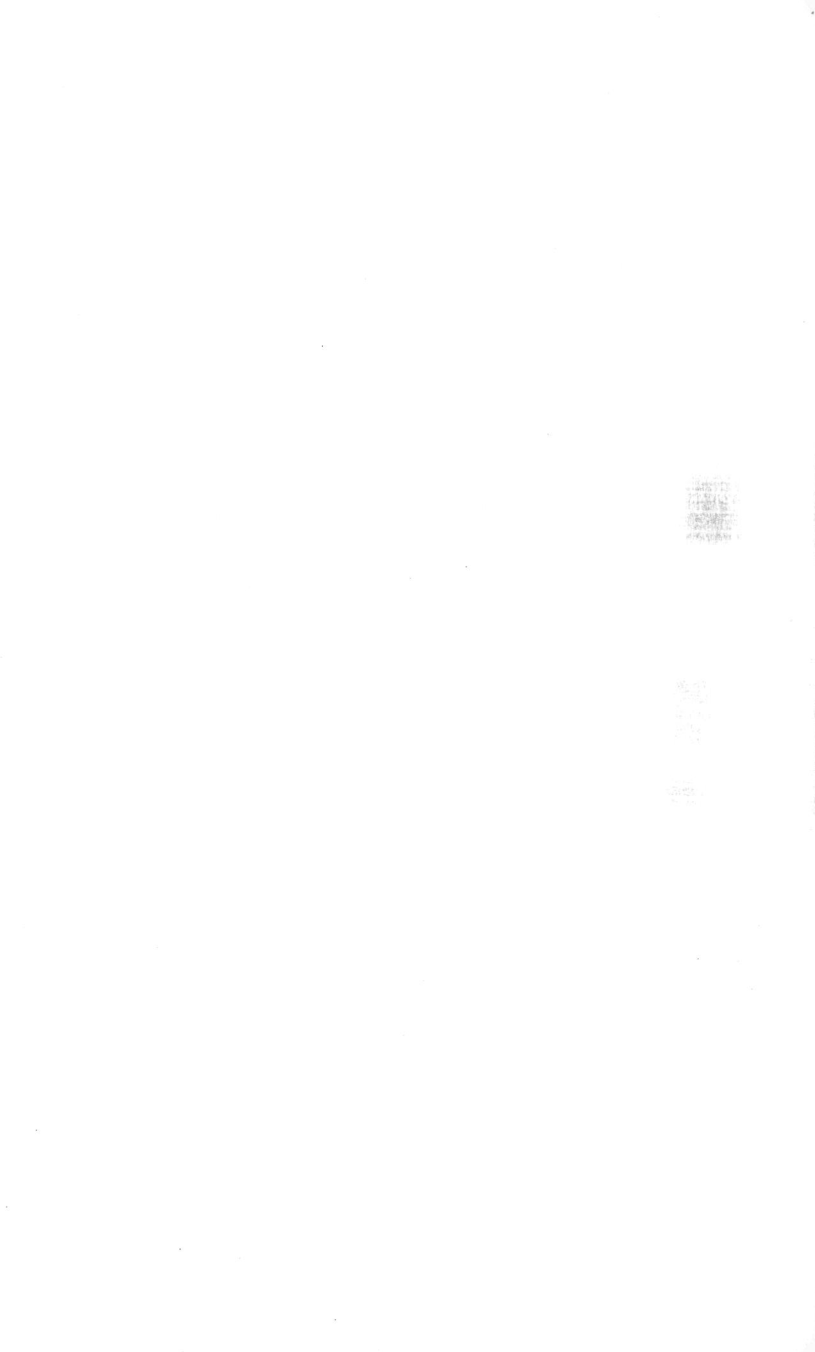